ALMIGHTY
OVER ALL

Other Books by R. C. Sproul Jr.

Dollar Signs of the Times: A Commonsense Guide to Securing Our Economic Future
Playing God (editor)
Vanity and Meaning (editor)

ALMIGHTY OVER ALL

Understanding
the Sovereignty of God

R. C. SPROUL JR.

Baker Books

A Division of Baker Book House Co
Grand Rapids, Michigan 49516

© 1999 by R. C. Sproul Jr.

Published by Baker Books
a division of Baker Book House Company
P.O. Box 6287, Grand Rapids, MI 49516-6287

Printed in the United States of America

Library of Congress Cataloging-in-Publication Data

Sproul, R. C. (Robert Craig), Jr., 1965–
    Almighty over all : understanding the sovereignty of
God / R. C. Sproul, Jr.
      p.   cm.
    ISBN 0-8010-5964-X (pbk.)
    1. Providence and government of God. I. Title.
BT96.2.S65   1999
231'.4—dc21   98-45470

For current information about all releases from Baker Book House, visit our web site:
                http://www.bakerbooks.com

To Darby, Campbell, Shannon, and Delaney,
and as many as are afar off

May you ever know the peace that comes from resting
on the omnipotent, strong right arm
of your heavenly Father.

CONTENTS

ACKNOWLEDGMENTS

Writing a book takes a lot of time. This one took longer than it should have. When I began the book, my wife, Denise, and I had one child. Now we have four, five if you count the book. And so it is appropriate that I thank my friends at Baker Book House first for their patience. Allan Fisher and Dan Van't Kerkhoff gently, kindly, understandingly encouraged me to keep going. I must also thank Brian Phipps, my editor. It is probably not every author he edits who is also an editor. Either that, or my pride may have made me a bit protective of the draft I turned in. But he took my baby and made her look better than I ever could. Any leftover cowlicks are my own fault.

I want also to thank the countless hundreds of friends who helped to sharpen my thinking on the sovereignty of God. I believe that education is conversation, and I learned too much from too many people to adequately thank everyone. The same is true for the great men with whom I've conversed who have already gone to their reward. Augustine, Aquinas, Luther, Calvin, Edwards, and Gerstner were my greatest teachers. But as with the editor, the mistakes remain my own.

Acknowledgments

Last, I'd like to thank my wife. While I was giving birth to a book on God's sovereignty, she was giving birth to the fruit of God's sovereignty, our four, so far, children. It is a taxing thing to care for small ones, but she was the first to say, "Why don't you go work on your book?"

To borrow an idiom from my friend George Grant, the sound track was provided by Palestrina, Bach, the Chieftans, and the beautiful and talented Mrs. Judy Rogers.

Reformation Day 1998
Meadowview, Virginia

10

All things in Scripture are not alike plain in themselves, nor alike clear unto all: yet those things which are necessary to be known, believed, and observed for salvation, are so clearly propounded, and opened in some place of Scripture or other, that not only the learned, but the unlearned, in a due use of the ordinary means, may attain unto a sufficient understanding of them.

Westminster Confession of Faith,
chapter 1, section 7

Introduction

How Strong Is He?

There are two common reactions to any discussion of the sovereignty of God, of the question of just how strong God is. I raise the subject in the form of a question asked in such basic terms in part to deflect the first reaction: Too often we flee such discussions. We reason that they are more often than not divisive to the body of Christ. We avoid the subject because it seems too abstruse for human study, too difficult to comprehend. Recognizing that we cannot know everything about God, we deem it arrogant to seek to know as much as we can about him. We tell ourselves it is like asking how many angels can pirouette atop a pin's head. A childlike faith, we reason, need not delve into theological questions involving such polysyllabic words as sovereignty, providence, and predestination.

It would seem, however, that a childlike faith would include a dominant quality of children: curiosity. Children want to know, they want their questions answered. "We are weak while he is strong," the children sing with the childlike affirmation, "Yes, Jesus loves me." "Well," a child might ask, "how strong is he?"

Children need to know the strength of those watching over them. "Daddy, make a muscle" was probably the most frequent request I gave my father when I was a child. I was impressed by his biceps, and comforted. I wanted to know that my dad had the strength to take on the most difficult challenges. When we read our children Bible stories, when they hear of the great flood or the parting of the Red Sea, they are gripped in part because these stories tell them something of how strong he is. A childlike faith ought to lead us to ask, and to seek to answer, How strong is he?

The second reaction is to be irresistibly drawn into debate. We feed on the friction of argument and drive any discussion into this arena. Predestination creeps its way into discussions on everything from the end times to the latest basketball scores. We may be quick to play the armchair Greek or Hebrew scholar, proving the axiom that a little knowledge is a dangerous thing. Answering the question, How strong is he? quickly becomes an exercise in How smart am I? Or worse still, How dumb are you? It's not surprising, then, that others don't want to play.

Neither reaction is a legitimate one. Any study of the character of God requires an appropriate understanding of our limited ability to know such things. Too little confidence and we miss the opportunity to know more about him; we fail to exhibit sufficient interest in him who can occupy our thought forever. Too much confidence and we become puffed up, interested less in him than in ourselves; our discussions work not to edify others but to impress them. Both land mines lurk just beneath the surface of this field of inquiry.

We can know things about God. To suggest that we cannot is to contradict oneself. If we say we can know nothing about God, we are actually saying we do know something about him: that he is unknowable. However, we do know things about God, because he has revealed them to us. He has, in his mercy, given us a glimpse of what lies behind the veil of his inscrutable glory. Our calling is to study that revelation with care, to draw as much information as possible from it without falling into the trap of dubious speculation. "To know, know, know him is to love, love, love him," the lady sang decades ago. It must follow that to love him is to know him. If we love him, we ought to want to know how strong he is, just as we ought to want to know how loving, how merciful, how patient he is. Our search to answer the question of his strength is the search to know him better. It is neither something to be ashamed of nor something for which we ought to be proud.

This area of inquiry especially ought to be one marked by humility. Any information on how strong he is reminds us how weak we are. Even our good desire to know him better is rooted not in our own goodness but in his almighty work in us. As we discover the depths of his strength, we are better able to rest in his arms. Let us stretch out our puny fingers to wrap them around the divine right arm and see what we can learn of our Father in heaven.

There is but one only, living, and true
God, who is infinite in being
and perfection, a most pure spirit,
invisible, without body, parts,
or passions. . . .

Westminster Confession of Faith,
chapter 2, section 1

1

WHO'S THERE?

Almighty from Eternity

Stop reading for a few seconds. Just a few seconds, please. Okay, you can read again. What happened while you waited? I'm going to make a wild guess that you asked yourself some variation of the question, Why did he ask me to stop? Probably the question you asked was more like, What in the world is this yahoo doing? Maybe you said to yourself, I'm no trained bear taking directions from a man I've never met; I'm going to keep reading.

That's fine. I wanted you to start a conversation with yourself. We all do it, and most of us never give it a thought, unless we start speaking aloud. As a child lying in my bed, I had intense conversations with myself in my mind that were stopped short when I began to wonder, To whom am I speaking? Of course, the conversations didn't stop; the subject just changed. I went from wondering if I would get a chance to ride my bike the next day to wondering about the nature of this internal conversation and who the participants are. Are there two of me? This in turn invariably raised the question that always frightened me: Which one is the real me? Am I the speaker or the listener?

I just discussed this with a young man. He suggested first that the listener is him. When I asked him who the speaker is, he puzzled for a moment and said, "That's me too. They're different parts of me."

The Unity and Simplicity of God

God, however, has no parts. He is a whole—a unity and a simplicity. The Westminster Confession of Faith asserts that God is "without parts." That concept is part of the most cherished element of the Old Testament confession. The Hebrews had as their central affirmation about God, their emblem of their faith, this statement from Deuteronomy: "Hear, O Israel, the LORD our God, the LORD is one (Deut. 6:4). This statement, known as the *shema,* was the unifying theme of the faith. No doubt when the Israelites gathered for chariot races there was always some guy in a rainbow wig carrying a sign that says, Deuteronomy 6:4.

So what's the big deal? We pass over this passage without giving it a second thought, without starting an internal conversation about it. To say that God is one or that he has no parts is to say that he cannot be divided. It reminds us that when we speak of God's attributes, we are making distinctions but not separating. God's sovereignty is not on his left side while his changelessness (immutability) is on his lower right. It's not as if the grace bone is connected to the love bone, and the love bone is connected to the omniscient bone. God is "of a piece." He is a unity, a whole. When we speak of his sovereignty, we do not set aside his grace, or vice versa. Too often when we get into disputes, we act not only as if God has parts but as if those parts are at war with each other. "Well," some say, "my God is a God of grace," as if a God of grace is somehow different from a God who is sovereign.

God does not have internal conversations the way you and I do. He cannot split himself up to hold up two ends of a conversation. And of course, because he is omniscient, because he knows all things, he neither retrieves information, moving it from some cob-webbed corner of his mind to his immediate consciousness, nor does he reason out answers. He has no questions for which he must recall or calculate the answers.

Neither is God's sovereignty something he must attain. When I remember my internal conversations from my youth, I am confronted with another puzzler. I asked then, Which one is me? I ask now, Which one of those voices in my five-year-old mind is now me? Have you ever considered the relationship between who you are now and who you were once before? Ten years ago the "I" who existed then vowed to be the last writer exclusively devoted to the legal pad. Yet the I who exists today writes on a computer. How are these I's related? I have changed, adapting to new technology, however reluctantly. But do you see the problem? To say I have changed is to assert both a continuity and a change. I am the same person I was, and I am not the same person. There is a continuity, a connection, between the former Luddite me and the current computer whiz me. Though I am a different person in the sense that I have acquired the willingness and the capacity to operate a computer and no longer have the fear I once had, I am still me. I have less hair, more pounds, but I am still me.

The ancient Greek philosophers wrestled with this problem (as did the apostle Paul in Romans 7). Some of the philosophers who lived before Socrates (most notably Parmenides) said that "whatever is, is." This view affirms that a chair is a chair and a man is a man, that things are what they are. This brilliant insight landed Parmenides a spot in the history of philosophy. Others, however (most notably Heraclitus), said that "whatever is, is becoming something else." They argued that change is at the root of all things. They affirmed that a chair was once a tree and a man was a boy, that whatever is was once something else and will one day be a third thing. They said that you cannot step into the same river twice. The river you first stepped into has changed, if only because the current carried the water that was in it at the time downstream. They would add, I presume, that you cannot step into the same puddle twice, not because the puddle changes but because you do. The you who first stepped in the puddle is different, if only because now you are a you with a wet shoe.

Of course, both schools of Greek thought are right, and both are wrong. All things stay the same in part, and all things change in part. The Greek philosophers called that which does not change the "being" and that which changes the "becoming." We are both continuity and change, being and becoming. There is a strong connection between the grown-up me and the five-year-old me. (Some complain that in my case the connection is too strong.) But there is also change.

Wait a minute! How did we get from a question about God's strength to a discussion of long dead Greeks? We took this brief side trip to understand better the awesomeness of God's being pure being. Parmenides was right about one thing, God. He is. What he is now, he always was and always shall be. In other words, there is no becoming in God; he is simply being. The root of God's strength is in this: God is.

God's sovereignty is not something he attained after eons of effort. He was never a ninety-seven-pound weakling who grew in strength after years of supporting the world on his shoulders. There are no before and after pictures of God Most High. God is absolutely sovereign now because he was absolutely sovereign from the beginning. Those Greek philosophers who asserted that "whatever is, is" were wrong because there is a sense in which we are and yet change. Those who asserted that "whatever is, is changing" were wrong because there is one thing which is not changing: God.

God doesn't change, because he is eternally one. And God is eternally one because he doesn't change. As confusing as that sounds, it underscores the great power of God's being a unity. To say that God changes is to affirm that part of God stays the same and part does not. But he has no parts. He is one. And because he cannot change, he is eternally one. He has always been one. If God "unified" parts of himself somewhere back in time such that he is now one, but once was not, then he would be mutable. But because he is immutable, he is all being, and no becoming.

When I consider my "isness," when I puzzle over the unchanging me, the continuity between the bicycle boy and the Macintosh man, I sometimes imagine myself as a string of pearls. The pearls represent the various attributes of me. One pearl is my love for my wife, another my love for my daughter. One pearl is my love of writing, another my aversion for vegetables. These, of course, change. I no longer love the Pittsburgh Pirates as I did as a boy. There once was a time when I didn't love my wife, because there was a time when I didn't know her. God willing, there will one day be many pearls for my love for my quiverful of children. What stays the same is the string on which the pearls hang. The same string that once held a pearl representing a love of bicycles now holds a pearl representing a love of Christ. That string is me, my being, while the pearls are my attributes, my becoming.

The string is still rather mysterious. I can't much describe it because it's just string. Whenever I try I usually end up describing one or more of the pearls. I have an especially hard time imagining what this string will look like in heaven when it is no longer weighed down by any sin. The string is something we don't see for all the pearls, but we know it's there, because something has to hold up those pearls.

Because God is pure being, no becoming, because he has no parts, we cannot conceive of him in the same way. God is pure string, no pearls. When we speak of the attributes of God, we are describing not pearls but the results of being pure string. The Bible teaches this in the way it speaks about God.

The Name of God

The Bible is overflowing with titles for God, descriptions of his various roles. He is called "my Provider," "Sovereign Ruler," "Father." But he has but one name.

You remember the story of when God revealed that sacred name. God commanded Moses to go and tell Pharaoh to release the captive Israelites in Egypt.

Moses asked who he should say sent him. At this point God offered not a title but a name, Yahweh. God did not say to tell Pharaoh that he was sent by a powerful God, or a merciful God, or a provider, or even a redeemer. God gave his sacred name, "I am."

Now Pharaoh was no dummy. He didn't need to wait for the Greeks to appear on the scene to help him understand the implications of this odd name. In fact, I suspect he would have been rather suspicious of Greeks bearing such strange philosophical gifts as the insight "Whatever is, is." This god of Moses, he knew, was not merely claiming to be a new god on the block. Moses didn't approach Pharaoh and warn him, "There's a new god in town, and this town ain't big enough for the both of you." He knew Moses was claiming to have a message from *the* God. (God, however, had a mind to keep Pharaoh acting rather stubbornly, but we'll deal with that later.)

"I am" or "I am that I am" says at least three things about God and his sovereignty. It suggests first that he is the one with the power of being. Because God is pure being, all other lesser beings are dependent upon him for their being. That which changes must be dependent upon that which doesn't change for being, because that which changes was once not. It must then have as its ultimate source that which always was, pure being. In claiming such a name, God is reminding all who hear it of what they already know, that without him they will pass straight into nonexistence. He is no mere Zeus who sends down thunderbolts which may or may not find their target. He is the source not only of the air we breathe, of the water we drink, but of the we. As easily as he could take away my pearls, he could destroy the string. God, on the other hand, is self-existent, not dependent on anyone or anything for his existence. Because he is pure being—unchanging and eternal—God is the only being who can never cease to be. The death of God theologians of the 1960s affirmed a contradiction. God, by definition, cannot cease to exist.

The second thing the name reveals is that God always was. For Pharaoh this meant not only that he had a new boss to deal with but that he, without knowing it, had always had this boss to deal with. He not only had to watch his step moving forward, he realized that all his previous steps had been under the watchful eye of Moses' god. Of course, Moses made the same horrifying discovery when he first heard the name issuing from the burning bush.

The third thing the name declares is God's unity. Since his unity is grounded in his self-existence, it is only fitting that his name would assert that unity. It is true he allows his attributes to be used to describe him, but through his name he asserts that he is string, being. All the attributes necessarily follow from being pure being.

"I am" is not a name meant to suggest "none of your business." I know we are tempted to read it as such. It seems as if Moses asks for God's name and God responds with, "Never mind who I am, the important thing is that I am." The point of the name, however, is not to veil the truth but to reveal it. It defines God.

A definition includes everything that should be included, while excluding all that should be excluded. If I define a horse as a four legged animal, I have given a poor definition; I have included too much. Based on that little bit of information one could conclude that a dog, a cat, a rat, and a pig are all horses. If, however, I define a horse as a brown, four-legged animal ridden by cowboys in rounding up cows, I have excluded not only white horses used to round up cows but brown horses used to pull plows.

"I am" avoids both problems. First, there is no other being that is pure being. We will never encounter a pure being that is not God. Second, we will never encounter God who is not pure being. Had God given as his name "he who is very strong," that would have been true enough, but it would have included the heavyweight boxing champ. If God had named himself "he who makes rocks so big he cannot move them," he would have excluded not only everyone else but also himself. (We will discuss very big rocks in a later chapter.)

Even God's name then tells us a great deal about how strong he is. In revealing his name to Moses, God made clear a vital truth. The apostle Paul, however, noted that this was really not newly revealed information. God's revelation of himself, while most clear in Scripture, is found not only in Scripture. It's not as if God waited until Moses sat down to write Genesis to tell his creatures about himself. And of course, it's not as if the only ones fortunate enough to know anything about God before Moses are those few blessed ancestors of ours who spoke to God, people like Noah, Abraham, and Jacob. God has revealed things about himself from the beginning, things seen and known by all. When Adam first breathed, had God been out for a walk, Adam would have realized quickly not only that there is a God but that he is all being and, hence, all power- ful. Not only would pure Adam have realized this in the garden, but all men, in their fallen state, looking at the fallen creation make the same discovery. Paul says in his letter to the church at Rome, "For since the creation of the world His invisible attributes are clearly seen, being understood by the things that are made, even His eternal power and Godhead, so that they are without excuse" (Rom. 1:20).

Do you notice the two things that are evident in the creation? Of course all men know that there is a God; they know of the Godhead in a vague sort of way. If you were walking through a forest and came across an acre of neatly tilled ground, rows of stakes holding up young tomato plants, and a scarecrow, you would know instantly that a gardener had been there. Unless you were Sherlock Holmes you wouldn't know if the gardener were male or female, tall or short, or what kind of cigar the gardener preferred. But you would know there is a gardener.

The universe, however, tells us important things about the Creator. Paul says all men know of his *eternal* power. One might expect Paul to say something about his infinite power. After all, it's much harder to create and sustain a whole universe than a small garden. It's a prodigious feat of strength. Paul, though, says eternal power. Eternal power is a power without a previous source. It is self-existent power, or the power of self-existence. It is the power of being pure being, a power that says "I am."

It pleased God the Father,
Son, and Holy Ghost,
for the manifestation
of the glory of his eternal power,
wisdom, and goodness,
in the beginning, to create, or make
of nothing, the world, and all things
therein whether visible or invisible,
in the space of six days;
and all very good.

Westminster Confession of Faith,
chapter 4, section 1

WHO'S WHERE?

Almighty over Nothing

Imagine nothing. Go ahead and give it a try. Come on, there's nothing to it. It shouldn't take long; there's not much to conjure in your mind when imagining nothing. Having difficulty? It is probably more difficult to imagine nothing than it is not to imagine pink elephants when discouraged from doing so. Nothing, in fact, is probably more of a puzzling concept than infinity. (After all, nothing is more complex than infinity.)

The problem with talking or thinking about nothing is that in doing so we invariably turn it into something. *Nothing* is a noun. It is not a person, and it is not a place (those would be no one and no where). It must then be a thing, but it can't be a thing, because it is no thing. Nothing is a noun that is not a person, place, or thing. When we speak or think of nothing, we are actually speaking or thinking about something, a concept. Writing about the concept is what I've been doing. Writing the thing itself would look like this:

The problem is that we often confuse the concept with the real thing. If I try to describe nothing, I would begin, "Nothing is . . ." and already I'm in deep weeds because nothing isn't.

We're going to try anyway, because nothing (the concept, not the reality) tells us something about how strong God is.

Let's go back to imagining nothing. If there were ever nothing, absolutely nothing, what would there be now? Nothing. Though the concept is difficult, one thing we can be absolutely sure of is that if there were ever a time when there was nothing, there would be nothing now. We have such confidence because of an iron rule of reason: *ex nihil, nihil fit,* out of nothing, nothing comes. That Latin phrase is just a reworking of the inviolable rule of logic that every effect must have a sufficient cause. "Something" is an effect, and if there were once nothing, there would not have been something to cause something else to be. Therefore, if there is something now, there must never have been nothing. There must have always been something that caused everything else to exist.

How, then, can the fact that there was never nothing tell us something about how strong God is? Because once there was God and nothing else. (Remember, though, that that's not two things. He was, while nothing else was. There was God, and everything else wasn't.) So God is so strong, he created something out of nothing.

In the Beginning

The Bible begins with this pregnant phrase: "In the beginning God." Most of us just rush right past these four words. We miss the weight of this beginning. We're impatient for the rest of the story. But if we'd slow down, we would see that this beginning raises another frustrating brainteaser. "In the beginning" suggests that there was no before. Moses, when he wrote Genesis, didn't begin with "Very early on" or "A long time ago." Time itself is a part of the creation. To speak of "before" the creation, then, creates problems, but it is unavoidable. How can we not speak this way? We often study history by moving backward through time. We ask, "What happened before that?" And when we are told we ask again, "Well, what happened before that?" What happens, then, when we ask what happened before time, before the beginning? Just like we want to know what is outside the edge of the universe, we want to know what happened before the beginning. Jonathan Edwards once proposed an answer to this question. When a man asked Edwards what God was doing before he made the world, Edwards answered, "Making Hell for the curious."

Because Moses began with "In the beginning," though, we have no biblical account of what happened before. There is no footnote on page one or appendix in the back of the book covering prehistoric history. All we can do is deduce a few things from what we know.

The first thing we know is that God was there. Though the doctrine of the Trinity is somewhat veiled in the Old Testament, we know that the Trinity is eternal. Father, Son, and Holy Spirit existed in a timeless state before time. There was no time when they were not, though there was a they when time was not.

So what were they doing? Enjoying each other's company. I know it seems rather undramatic, but that's only because our enjoyment of the company of others pales in comparison with the joy of the Trinity. The communion of the Trinity is a deep and profound communion. It is the foundation of true love; it is the model of which our relationships are only faint copies. The three persons of the Godhead enjoyed (and, of course, now and will forever enjoy) a full, total, and intimate knowledge of one another. This is not a love born of mystery, a love that might be damaged by future knowledge. This is not a love born of wish projection, of imposing lovable qualities on the object of affection. The love which binds together the deity is a perfect love. The joy, then, that flows from this love is likewise perfect, not lacking in anything, complete.

This love is not damaged by a failure by either the loved or the loving. The Father does not think, "I love the Son, but I would love him more if only he would quit that annoying habit of his." This love is not tarnished by jealousy. The Son is not envious of the Father's position. No member of the Trinity needs to be sanctified to garner a deeper capacity to love. The lovers are as infinite in their capacity to love as the loved are infinitely lovable.

Neither is there some external lack which might diminish their capacity to love one another. Because I must go out into the world to provide for my family, we have less time together in which we might learn to love each other more. Because I might become frustrated with my work, I might become irritable and that much less lovable. The Trinity, however, lacks nothing. The persons of the Trinity have nothing (the real lack of things, not the concept) to distract them.

The complete joy of the Godhead is a foreign concept to us. In our therapeutic age we cannot comprehend any being without needs. We comfort ourselves with the idea that God has needs just like you and I. But the Westminster Confession of Faith presents a much hardier God than our rather feeble, needy God, and the Westminster writers likewise had a much hardier faith. In chapter 2 of the Confession they list some of the attributes of God. Section 2 of the chapter begins, "God hath all life, glory, goodness, blessedness, in and of himself; and is alone in and unto himself all-sufficient, not standing in need of any creatures which he hath made. . . ." Those are strong words describing a strong God. This teaching is drawn from God's self-revelation, the Bible. Paul, in his grief over the unbelief of the Israelites, says of them, "Of whom are the fathers and from whom, according to the flesh, Christ came, who is over all, the eternally blessed God" (Rom. 9:5). Here Paul affirms not only the deity of Christ but a necessary characteristic of deity, eternal blessedness. Paul is not merely saying that now, after the incarnation, after his ascension to the throne of glory, is Christ blessed, but that he has always been blessed. He is eternally blessed. That means Jesus, in his deity, enjoyed a fullness of blessedness before time, when there was only the Godhead and nothing else.

We now face something of a dilemma. If we are persuaded that God was blessed, that he experienced an unlimited joy, that he lacked absolutely nothing, we must ask why he bothered to create the world. It would seem that God who lacks nothing would lack at least this: a reason to create the universe. Of course, there is no escape the other way. If we say that God created the world out of some lack, if we accept the common wisdom that God somehow was lonesome or wanted for human companionship, then we reduce God to something less than sovereign. Loneliness would have reigned supreme before the creation.

But God, of course, has no lack. Yet we know he did in fact create the universe. So what was his motivation, since he lacks nothing? This question is one over which theologians have wrestled fiercely in the history of the church. It is called the "full bucket" problem. Before creation, God's "bucket" was full. He lacked nothing. So why did he act? The traditional solution to this vexing question turns the problem on its head; it turns the bucket upside down. Theologians have reasoned that God created because of the fullness of his bucket, because of the fullness of his glory. The reason for the creation in God's case was not a lack but a fullness. God's glory overflowed the bucket. It needed an arena, a theater for its display, and thus the creation came to pass. It is for this reason David says, "The heavens declare the glory of God . . ." (Ps. 19:1). The whole of creation exists to speak, to tell a story, the simple yet immeasurably profound story that God is indeed glorious.

To whom is the story told? The glory of God shown forth by the creation is told in part to the creation, particularly to the pinnacle of that creation, man. We should be careful to remember, however, that while the message gets through to man and is vital to him, man does not stand above the creation. Man is himself a part of that creation and thus ultimately is not the reason for the creation. The telling forth of God's glory ultimately is done for God's pleasure. The story is told by

God, for God. Mankind is a critical part of that story, and man alone among the earthly creatures can have some grasp of it, but the story is not for man but for God. It is because God delights in both the telling and the witnessing of the story that the story is told.

Contradiction and Paradox

How does the story begin? That brings us back to the beginning, to Moses' pregnant words, "In the beginning God created the heavens and the earth." We stated earlier that we know there was never a time when God was not or when nothing was because of the iron law of logic, *ex nihil, nihil fit,* out of nothing, nothing comes. That phrase might sound vaguely familiar. Christians throughout the centuries have affirmed the doctrine of creation *ex nihilo,* out of nothing. I once had a conversation with a Christian who was a professor of philosophy. He was struggling with this doctrine. To him, affirming both creation *ex nihilo* and *ex nihil, nihil fit* is to affirm a contradiction. A contradiction is when we affirm two different things which cannot both be true. The problem with affirming a contradiction, of course, is that to do so is to affirm a falsehood. It is always true of a contradiction that at least one of the affirmations is false.

Now, it might be tempting, when delving into the often mysterious study of creation, of being, of time, to accept contradictions as true. God, we reason, is infinite. He is wiser than us, and mysterious. Being infinite, we think, he can reconcile contradictions so that both elements can be true. Perhaps, we think, these ideas of creation out of nothing, and nothing coming from nothing are like two parallel lines that intersect in infinity.

Such thinking has several advantages. It certainly seems pious, dripping with humility. It certainly can make our lives easier, in that we don't have to wrestle through difficult problems. And doesn't it just glorify God, making him so much bigger than silly human reason? But there's a problem. If these two propositions are like two parallel lines that intersect in infinity, then they are like two lines that never intersect that do intersect. If two lines do intersect and don't intersect, then it would seem to follow that God could be gracious and not be gracious, that he could be good and evil, that he could be all-powerful and have no power.

If we can't rely on contradiction to alert us to falsehood, then there can be no falsehood. If there is no falsehood, there can be no truth. If there is no truth, you might as well put this book down now, because you are wasting your time. Of course, if contradictions can be true, you wouldn't want to put the book down, because though reading it is a waste of your time, it is also an investment of your time in the most profitable manner. So what are you going to do? If two parallel lines intersect anywhere, then you won't ever know what to do. One choice is as good and as bad as another. (We will look at the relation of God and logic more fully in chapter 9.)

Is there a way, then, other than affirming contradictions, by which we can help our professor friend? There is. Remember that every effect must have a sufficient cause. That is why nothing comes from nothing. With respect to creation there is a sufficient cause, God. The doctrine of creation *ex nihilo* teaches not that the universe was created by nothing but that it was created from nothing. It affirms not that there was no cause but that there were no materials. To say that out of nothing, nothing comes and that God created the universe out of nothing is to speak a paradox, not a contradiction. A paradox is a statement which appears to contradict itself but which upon examination is found to be true. When Jesus said, "Whoever loses his life will find it and whoever finds his life will lose it," he was not speaking a contradiction but a paradox. Jesus was teaching that whoever would lose his life in one sense would gain it in another. In like manner, when we affirm creation *ex nihilo* we are using the phrase in a different manner than when we affirm *ex nihil, nihil fit*. If creation *ex nihilo* means creation by nothing, it would mean that God turned around one day and there was a universe, much to his surprise. On the contrary, creation *ex nihilo* means there was a prior cause, but no prior materials.

There is, of course, still quite a bit of room left for awe. Something by nothing is impossible; something out of nothing is amazing.

We have to be careful how we talk of creation out of nothing for another reason. Not only is it easy to think of nothing as some kind of thing, it's easy to think of it as a place. When we say that God called forth the light out of nothing, the tendency is to believe that the light was waiting around in this place called nothing, waiting for its appearance on the stage. He didn't move the universe into existence. He didn't summon it; he created it.

That is how strong God is. When he commands something to happen, it does. He is no mere craftsman who takes what is and reshapes it. I can enter a dark room and declare, "Let there be light." But if I want my command to have any effect, I must flip a switch, which lets loose a stream of electricity, which travels until it arrives in the filament of a lightbulb, which in turn excites electrons such that the filament glows, throwing off energy in the form of light. God just speaks and it comes to pass.

Remember also that before, there was no such thing as light. When I want to "create" light, I have a good idea what it is, what it looks like. Edison knew quite a bit about light before making a device to bring it forth at will. God not only created the light, he created the idea of light, the concept.

God also called forth matter. He took the idea of matter and spoke it into existence. Space and time are his too. All those elements of the created order which continue to baffle our best minds, he not only understands fully but also made. The intricacies of creation, from the unfathomable wonder of the galaxies, to the mystery of the human mind and body, to the dizzying dance of subatomic particles, are astounding enough. That he ordered and arranged and sustains all of this should knock us over. But even more incredible is that he created it all.

How strong is he? Strong enough that from before time he determined to create a universe to show forth his strength and glory. He is so strong that the universe cannot contain his strength. He is so strong that whatever he speaks immediately comes to pass. There is no struggle with God, no exertion. He burned no calories, pulled no muscles, strained no ligaments in his act of creation. On the seventh day he "rested," but he is ever at work. He did not stop manifesting his strength at the creation, but continues in history.

God, from all eternity, did,
by the most wise and holy counsel
of his own will, freely,
and unchangeably ordain
whatsoever comes to pass. . . .

Westminster Confession of Faith,
chapter 3, section 1

3

WHO DUNIT?

Almighty in Authority

Everybody loves a mystery story. At least everybody should love a mystery story. Okay, I love a mystery story. My wife, as a gift for our first Saint Valentine's Day after we were married, gave me, in one volume, the complete collection of Sherlock Holmes mysteries. I didn't devour the book; I savored it. Each night before going to sleep I would read one story, and one story only. As is common in most mystery tales, each story has a few simple elements. A crime is committed. A list of suspects is introduced, and then slowly that list is narrowed until the culprit is found. With careful logic Holmes investigates who had a motive, who had opportunity, and who had the means.

Though Holmes rarely worked this way, it is not uncommon in a mystery story for all the suspects to be confined to a small area. The same storm which apparently knocked out the lights before the murder forces the guests at the manor on the island to stay put. We find that young master Conrad, the playboy nephew, is about to be cut out of the old man's will. We learn that Jeeves the butler is about to be fired because the master learned of his secret wife and family living in the slums of London.

In theology, mysteries are not so different. We must work with what facts we know and seek to reason out the best possible answer. In the previous chapter, we tried to understand creation by affirming both that God is eternal and that the material world is not. Some people are too comfortable with mysteries. Any time there is a little puzzle, these folks throw up their hands and gladly declare, "Mystery," thereby avoiding the labor of unraveling it. Such false humility has the added advantage of seeming pious. The problem is that when we give up our search for understanding too early, we miss out on opportunities to know better who God is and what he has done. If, because I don't understand how a lightbulb works, I merely declare its operation a mystery too grand for me, then when the bulb burns out, I won't know that simply by replacing the bulb I can have light again. I'm afraid I'd be more silly than pious sitting in a dark room.

Perhaps no mystery has puzzled theologians more than the problem of evil.

The two theologians whose thought I know and admire the most—men who are loathe to cry mystery—when asked where evil comes from (and they are asked often), give the same unsatisfactory answer: they shrug their shoulders.

They're not alone in being puzzled. The problem of evil has vexed the greatest minds of history, inside and out of the Christian church. By the problem of evil I do not mean how we explain why bad things happen to people. That's not such a big problem once you come to recognize that all men are sinners and deserve only death. The difficult question is how men came to be sinners in the first place. Remember that there once was God and nothing else. Now there is not only God and the universe but also evil. Where did it come from?

To chip away at this problem, we will approach it like detectives solving a mystery.

The Suspects

In the Garden of Eden we have an ideal case for investigation. Like the guests on the island manor, we are dealing with a limited geographic area and, of course, a limited number of suspects.

Who are the suspects? On whom can we pin the blame for the introduction of evil into the world? There are five possibilities: Adam, Eve, Satan, God, and the birds and the bees and the rocks and the trees. This last group might seem a little puzzling. After listing all the personal moral agents—beings capable of moral behavior—we should include the possibility that the blame could be pinned on the impersonal matter present at the scene.

What was the situation before the crime? Adam and Eve had been created by God, who had declared his creation "good." They lived in a garden paradise, vice-regents over the created order under God. They walked with God and talked with him. They enjoyed fellow-

45

ship with God and with each other. They had nothing to fear. They were at peace and were comfortable in their surroundings. They had everything they needed. And suddenly, there was sin.

As we enter the crime scene, like all good investigators we will question first those who were present when the crime was committed. So let's look at Eve. She certainly was present, and so had opportunity. The next question is whether she had the means. Did Eve have it in her power to create sin? To answer that question we need to learn a lesson from the greatest analytical mind ever to grace the American scene—Jonathan Edwards. This gentleman's intellect makes Holmes look like a dolt. Another Holmes, Supreme Court jurist Oliver Wendell Holmes, not one to carry a brief for orthodox Christianity, said of Edwards that his was the greatest mind of the last two hundred years.

Edward's most enduring and influential work was his lengthy essay, "The Freedom of the Will." The argument he makes in this essay can be used to prove conclusively that Eve could not be the culprit, for she had not the means. The argument is surprisingly simple. Edwards wrote that all men everywhere always act according to their strongest inclination at a given time.

Stop to consider whether there was ever a time when you acted against your strongest inclination. If you were like most kids, when you were told to eat your vegetables, you certainly weren't inclined to eat them. But if you in fact ate the vegetables, that must have been your strongest inclination at the time. It's true that fear of a whack on the seat of your pants might have been part of the equation, but given your choices, eating vegetables was the strongest of the two inclinations at the time. Even when the choices are unpleasant, we choose.

Jack Benny illustrated this in a routine in which he was approached by a thug who said, "Your money or your life." A pregnant pause followed until Benny explained, "I'm thinking, I'm thinking." Of course, there are times when we are the victims of violence and don't really make choices. Most muggers, when they say, "Your money or your life," actually mean, "Your money, or your money and your life." As with taxes, there is no option which lets you keep your money.

I've asked hundreds of people who have difficulty with this concept to give an example in which they chose to do something other than their strongest inclination. Each and every time the choice may not have been what was desired, all things being equal, but things are never equal. Edwards was right; we always choose according to our strongest inclination given our choices.

Consider, then, Eve. She was in the garden when the serpent approached her. He began the dialogue with a question, "Has God indeed said, 'You shall not eat of every tree of the garden'?" (Gen. 3:1). Eve corrected the serpent, explaining that she is free to eat of any tree save one. She then erred, adding to God's restriction by saying she must not even touch the fruit, lest she die. So far she has erred but is without sin. The serpent then directly contradicted God by declaring, "You will not surely die" (Gen. 3:4).

So Eve considered the fruit. She weighed her options. The text tells us she recognized that the fruit was good for food, that it was pleasing to the eye, and that it was desirable to be wise. And so she ate. But she couldn't have eaten on her own. Remember God had earlier made a declaration concerning Eve: "Then God saw everything that He had made, and indeed it was very good" (Gen. 1:31). If Eve was good, this must mean that her inclination was only good. Remember Jesus, who alone was good, said, "My food is to do the will of Him who sent Me, and to finish His work" (John 4:34). Goodness, at least with respect to personal moral agents, means the desire to obey God. Certainly God couldn't call good that which has anything other than the desire to obey and please him. To be good is to have only good inclinations, to have a good nature. And can someone who is good do bad? Someone far more astute than Edwards said no in the most famous sermon of all time, "You will know them by their fruits. Do men gather grapes from thornbushes or figs from thistles? Even so, every good tree bears good fruit, but a bad tree bears bad fruit. A good tree cannot bear bad fruit, nor can a bad tree bear good fruit" (Matt. 7:16–18).

So we have a problem. According to what Jesus said, if Eve was good, she couldn't have done bad. God said that Eve was good, and yet she did bad. The only conclusion we can reach is that at some time between God's pronouncement of Eve's goodness and the eating of the fruit, she had to stop being good. So what or who changed Eve's inclination?

This is the real crime. The eating of the fruit, if you will, is the fruit of a crime which had already taken place. Did Eve change her inclination from good to bad? Fortunately for Eve, she cannot be guilty. She cannot be the one who changed her inclination, because she didn't have the means. She didn't have the means because she didn't have a motive.

Eve was by the tree, contemplating whether she would change her inclination from good to bad. Her inclination at the time was good. Is it a good thing or a bad thing to change one's inclination from good to bad? For Eve to have as her strongest inclination the inclination to change from good to bad, she would have had to be bad. She could not have changed her own inclination any more than a leopard can change its spots or a good tree can bear bad fruit. We must excuse Eve from our investigation. Something outside of her must have been the agent of change, that which changed her inclination from good to bad. Though she was the one who first ate of the tree, she cannot be the one who introduced evil into the world.

How about Adam? Could he have been the one to change Eve's inclination? He certainly had opportunity. He too was in the garden. He had authority over Eve. The problem, of course, is that Adam also fell under God's blessing. He too was part of the creation that God declared to be good. He too, then, must have had the inclination only to do good. Is it a good inclination to desire to change Eve's inclination from good to bad? Adam, being good, could have had no desire to change Eve. And when we add that Adam doesn't have the power to change Eve, he slips quickly off the suspect list. Humans haven't the power to change the inclination of other humans. This lack of power is not the result of the fall but is inherent in man's nature.

That same lack of power applies to our strange suspect, the birds and the bees and the rocks and the trees. Though these things were present at the commission of the crime, they too have neither a motive nor the power. These things are impersonal. They do not influence the desires of humans. They have no consciousness, so they couldn't have chosen to change Eve. And if they had consciousness, just how would they have effected their desire? While I may wish that it is the candy bar which woos me, calls me to break my diet, candy bars don't talk. And neither do rocks.

This leads us to the crowd favorite. All of us, I'm sure, are hoping we can pin this dastardly deed on the serpent in the black hat. We don't much care for him, and we know he is destined to a rather lengthy jail term anyway. It sure would be nice if we could pin this crime on him and solve one more mystery.

There are, however, several problems with this suspect. While it is true that he was at the scene of the crime and had opportunity and a motive, he cannot be the culprit.

Though the devil, unlike the rocks and the trees, is personal, he too hasn't the power to change the inclination of humans. Though incredibly powerful, he is yet a creature. Though he can and does tempt and seduce, he always does so by appealing to our already twisted inclinations. We have one example in which Satan tried to work his devilry with someone who had no inclination to do evil. Three times Satan sought to twist Jesus' legitimate desires into sinful desires. There is nothing inherently wrong with desiring to eat, especially after fasting forty days, so Satan said, "If You are the Son of God, command that these stones become bread" (Matt. 4:3). Jesus' strongest inclination, however, was to obey his Father, and so he refused. So Satan said, "If You are the Son of God, throw Yourself down" (v. 6). Again Jesus' strongest desire was to obey God. Finally Satan said, "All these things I will give You if You will fall down and worship me" (v. 9). Jesus knew that all things rightfully would be his; yet again his strongest inclination was to obey God.

In the garden, Satan tried to get Eve to see things differently. He tried to appeal to her natural and legitimate desire to know more. He could not, however, make that desire surpass the fundamental desire of those who are good, the desire to obey God's commands. Satan, then, could not be the culprit.

Even if Satan could have been the culprit, it still wouldn't really solve our problem of where evil came from. Even if Eve rightly could say, "The devil made me do it," we must then push the question further back. How could the devil come to be evil? Like Adam and Eve, the devil was created good. There was a time when his desires were only to obey God. Blaming the devil does not ultimately help us in solving the mystery. The devil, as the angel of light, before his fall, could not have had the inclination to do evil either.

Some try to pin this on the devil by suggesting that he allowed a legitimate desire to grow into an illegitimate desire. Still, there must have been a time when that good desire approached that line. The devil had a choice; would he allow this desire to grow into sin or not? To desire to allow it to so grow would again require an inclination toward evil, an inclination the devil could not yet have had.

The Culprit

Who are we left with? The case against God, the argument that he must be the one who introduced evil into his world, does not rest merely on the process of elimination. Let us, with great care and respect, apply to God the same method in our search for the source of evil as we have applied to our other suspects.

We know that God was present. We know this at least because there is no place where he was not. God can never use as an alibi that he was somewhere else, because while he is somewhere else, he is also always present everywhere. So God at least had the opportunity.

Did God have the means? Of course he did. He is God; he can do whatever he wishes. There is no power greater than him which could somehow stop him from changing Eve's inclination. We know also that it not only is possible for God to change a person's inclination, we know that in fact it is his habit to do so. He does it all the time. In fact, he has done it to me. And if you are a servant of his, we know he has done it to you. After the fall, the Bible teaches, our strongest inclination at any given moment is always to sin. The only way this process can be arrested, such that anyone could come to faith, is if God sovereignly changes our inclination first. (We will discuss this in greater depth in a later chapter.)

The next question, then, is to ask if God had a motive for changing Eve's inclination. What reason would God have for wanting Eve to fall into sin? Imagine God before the creation of the world. The members of the Trinity are enjoying the fellowship of which we spoke earlier. They are noting their excellencies, praising each other, if you will. God considers his strength and finds it wonderful. He considers his mercy and finds it delightful. And then he considers his wrath. Many of us have difficulty imagining God finding any glory in his wrath, but he does. He is pleased with his wrath. If his wrath exists, and we know from his Word that it does, then we know he is pleased with it. We cannot imagine God looking at his wrath like unwanted pounds he wants to lose, if only he had the power. No, God is as delighted with his wrath as he is with all of his attributes. Suppose he says, "What I'll do is create something worthy of my wrath, something on which I can exhibit the glory of my wrath. And on top of that I'll manifest my mercy by showering grace on some of these creatures deserving my wrath." Can you imagine God thinking such a thought? I can, and I'm not alone in this. The apostle Paul not only speculates that such a line of reasoning is possible with God but that in fact God did reason this way. "What if God, wanting to show His wrath and to make His power known, endured with much longsuffering the vessels of wrath prepared for destruction, and that He might make known the riches of His glory on the vessels of mercy, which He had prepared beforehand for glory, even us whom He called, not of the Jews only, but also of the Gentiles?" (Rom. 9:22–24).

These are perhaps some of the hardest words to swallow in all of Scripture. We could be sure, however, even without this passage that God would have a motive for Eve's fall into sin. We know that, because it came to pass. Every Bible-believing Christian must conclude at least that God in some sense desired that man would fall into sin. The only other option is to say that this event became reality against God's wishes, that God sat upon his throne wringing his hands in frustration as Eve took a bite. Such a notion is repugnant, for it means that someone or something is more powerful than God himself.

God wills all things which come to pass. It is in his power to stop whatever might come to pass. It is within his omniscience to imagine every possible turn of events and to choose that chain of events which most pleases him. What option most pleases him? It is always that option which gives him the most glory. Like man, God's chief end is to glorify God and enjoy him forever. And like man, God always acts according to his strongest inclination. What is different is that with God all things are equal in the sense that his choices are never limited. I must say, "Given that I must either eat these vegetables or receive a spanking . . ." But God, being all powerful, never finds himself in the unenviable position of having to choose among the lesser of two evils.

It is because of this similarity (God always acting according to his strongest inclination) and this difference (God always getting exactly what he wants) that we can know that whatever comes to pass must be what God most wished to come to pass, his strongest inclination.

But wait a minute. Isn't there an obvious argument against this line of reasoning? Isn't it impossible for God to do evil? Of course it's impossible for God to do evil. He can't sin. This objection, however, is off the mark. I am not accusing God of sinning; I am suggesting that he created sin. There is a difference.

We must define our terms. The Westminster Confession of Faith defines sin as "any lack of conformity to or transgression of the law of God." Where, I must ask, does the law of God forbid the creation of evil? I would suggest that it just isn't there. Someone might object that of course it isn't there, because man hasn't the power to create sin. And I would rest my case.

Somehow, though, it just doesn't seem fair of God to bring evil into the world and then turn around and express his wrath against it. One could just hear this complaint from people who want to defend God against the charge that he created evil. Were there a trial, they would have character witnesses come forth and explain that God is a fair God, a just God. And the underlying assumption would be that fairness and justice would keep God from changing Eve's inclination and then turning around and punishing her for acting on that inclination. Such an action would be an evil action by God, and therefore could not have happened. Treating Eve this way would be inconsistent with his character.

The prosecution, however, those trying to prove that it was God who changed Eve's inclination, if it were permitted to introduce similar activities of God performed elsewhere, would have an answer. The Bible clearly affirms that it was God who hardened the heart of Pharaoh: "For this purpose I have raised you up, that I may show My power in you, and that My name might be declared in all the earth" (Exod. 9:16). Here we have God doing two troublesome acts. First he raised up Pharaoh. It was God himself who put this tyrant in power, to rule over Abraham's children with an iron fist. And second he hardened Pharaoh's heart. Have you ever wondered how a man could be as stubborn as Pharaoh? Destruction rained down on his kingdom like cats and dogs, or like gnats and frogs. But he did not relent. Why? Because God had hardened his heart. Should Pharaoh be judged for these things? When he stands before the judgment throne of God, will he be able to say, "Hey, it's not my fault. For who can resist your will?" (And Eve, if she is still awaiting trial, might shout from the gallery a loud amen!)

He can certainly try that. But if Paul were in the courtroom (and he at least presented a "friend of the court" brief in his letter to the Romans), we can expect him to stand quickly and shout, "Objection!" He would surely go on to say, "But indeed, O man, who are you to reply against God? Will the thing formed say to him who formed it, 'Why have you made me like this?' Does not the potter have power over the clay, from the same lump to make one vessel for honor and another for dishonor?" (Rom. 9:20–21).

Notice Paul's argument assumes it was God who worked in the heart of Pharaoh. Paul does not say, "Hey Pharaoh, leave God out of this. He had nothing to do with you hardening your heart." Neither, ultimately, does Paul give a comfortable defense of God. The objection assumes God acts to ensure, through his work, that evil will be done. If you aren't inclined to shout, "That's not fair," then you are not understanding what Paul is saying. Paul's defense is essentially, "Shut up! He's God, and he can do what he wants."

It's as if Paul is saying this sham trial has gone on long enough. He is reminding us that the ultimate problem with putting God on trial is that God is the ultimate judge. All the while he was sitting in the seat of the accused, he had every right to stand up, bump the judge from his spot, and resume his rightful place. He alone is judge over all the earth.

If, then, the judge of all the earth finds it in his best interests—finds it to be that which glorifies him the most—to harden Pharaoh's heart, to ensure that Pharaoh will act stubbornly so God might work wonders before and for his people, he can do that. He does not merely wait for it to happen. He does not merely hope it will happen. He does not merely see ahead of time that it will happen. He makes sure it happens. He planned for it to happen, and he set things up to ensure that it would happen.

He can, if he wants, hire someone to make it happen. If it is his desire, he can hire a character assassin. God could have, and might have, summoned his servant Satan. He might have said, "Satan, go on down there and get to work in Pharaoh. Make him mean, plenty mean. I've got a plan I'm working on."

But even if God works through secondary causes—hires someone else to do his work for him—he cannot cease to be the primary cause. In a human trial, we recognize that hiring a hit man does not shift the blame from the hirer to the hiree. Both the trigger man and whoever ordered the hit stand trial for the crime. And both can hang for it.

The same could apply to Adam and Eve and the fall. God might not have operated on Eve personally. He might not have flipped the switch, changing her inclinations from good to evil. He must, however, have been the ultimate cause. He could have set things up in advance, arranged the possibilities such that it would happen. But as the sole creator and controller of those possibilities, the trail ultimately leads back to God.

It was his desire to make his wrath known. He needed, then, something on which to be wrathful. He needed to have sinful creatures. He wanted to make his mercy known. He needed, then, something that deserved wrath on which he could show mercy instead. All of this serves his eternal and ultimate desire, to glorify himself.

Somehow, though, this doesn't seem quite so glorifying, does it? Somehow we think that this smears his character more than it reveals his glory. Did he make a mistake? Did he, in trying to manifest his glory, instead somehow diminish it? Of course not.

Often when we think of God's glory we think of those things which impress us. We look out at a range of mountains, or a giant redwood tree, and think, "Wow, God, you sure are great to be able to make such beautiful things." When a new baby is born we are reminded of God's glory. These are all legitimate responses to God's glorious works. The problem is that we praise him more because we like what he has done, because it benefits us, than because he is pleased with it. His glorification of himself is not ultimately dependent on our reaction of awe. It is his own reaction that matters. If he is pleased, then he is glorified, even if we think it's not so great. We don't often think, for instance, of the glory God receives from the torment of souls in hell. We are willing to jump up and down praising God when he redeems a sinner, but when he damns one, we look away. Our problem is that we identify more with, or rather root more for, our fellow humans than for God. We are not as offended at sin as God is. We don't recognize the beauty of his wrath and so miss the glory in the execution of his wrath.

Naturally, then, we're going to have a terribly difficult time trying to see the glory in his bringing to pass the fall. Nevertheless, we ought to see the glory. We ought to jump up and down praising God for his strength, that he alone has the power and authority to change the inclinations of moral agents. More important, perhaps, we ought to be jumping up and down for the sublime wisdom of his plan. It is an incredible plan. He creates a world. He stamps his image upon two of his creatures. He declares them to be good. He then changes their inclination, either directly or indirectly, such that they fall into sin. That discordant note, however, resolves in an even greater harmony. For out of that very fall, he will exercise his wrath and show his mercy. And how will he show his mercy and yet remain just? That is the glorious story of the incarnation, the crucifixion, the resurrection, and the ascension.

All these events in Eden were so that the Son might glorify the Father and the Spirit, that the Spirit might glorify the Son and the Father, and that the Father might glorify the Spirit and the Son. It all hinges on the fall, on the changing of Eve's (and Adam's) inclination from good to bad, an event which was, on the one hand, a terrible tragedy but, on the other, the means by which God might be glorified.

All the rest of history, not just biblical or church history, but all history, is the unfolding of this plan, of his plan. It is the story of his acting for his glory. He acts not to impress us, not to make us happy and comfortable, but to manifest his awesome strength and authority. And that is what we will continue to explore. He is sovereign; there's no great mystery in that.

*The almighty power, unsearchable
wisdom, and infinite goodness
of God so far manifest themselves
in his providence, that it extendeth
itself even to the first fall, and all
other sins of angels and men;
and that not by a bare permission,
but such as hath joined with it
a most wise and powerful bounding,
and otherwise ordering,
and governing of them,
in a manifold dispensation,
to his own holy ends. . . .*

Westminster Confession of Faith,
chapter 5, section 4

WHO'S DRIVING?

Almighty over History

It is arrogant to presume to predict the future. It is clever, however, to predict the future in one's own favor. Consider the work of Karl Marx. Because of our ignorance of history, and our tendency to telescope history (to push events closer together than they really are), we often connect Marx with the Russian Revolution of 1917. We think of him like a Moses, who looked into the Promised Land and just barely missed seeing his dream become reality. The truth is that Marx died dozens of years before the revolution. Yet as he wrote of his beloved system in the safety and comfort of a library in London, he made an astonishing prediction. He wrote not only that he hoped for a worldwide worker's revolution, not only that he thought such was likely to take place, but that such a revolution was absolutely certain to happen, that it was historically inevitable. The arrogance in such a brash claim is obvious, but where is the cleverness? The claim served as a principal motivation to the very workers he hoped would bring about the revolution. When any of us are faced with a daunting task (and there are few more daunting than worldwide revolution), it helps if we are persuaded that our victory is secure.

Of course, Marx looks pretty silly right now, with his system being practiced with much care in only a very few countries. But such is the end of arrogance, even clever arrogance. Across time there have been assorted other predictions of a bright future. Intellectuals during the Enlightenment period, though they rarely developed a system as radical as that of Marx's, operated under the same optimistic view of the destiny of mankind. They were quite confident that with the right application of the scientific method, whether it be through technology, education, or environment, utopia was within their grasp.

The future, however, has a way of eluding us. It is under the control of neither revolutionaries nor technocrats. That doesn't mean, however, that history is random. The failures of a host of Western "isms" should not drive us to an Eastern view of history in which time is just spinning its wheels. History is moving, progressing—and progressing to a certain end. That end is reflected in a sign on a church near my home. It reads, "We know the future—God wins!"

It might seem an odd time in this book to pick up this theme. How can we turn from the puzzling horror of the fall of man to the good news of God's triumph and sovereignty over history? We do so because the Bible does. Immediately after the fall of man we are given a vision of the future: "And I will put enmity between you and the woman, and between your offspring and hers; he will crush your head, and you will strike his heel" (Gen. 3:15 NIV). Like Marx, God declares there will be a struggle that will last through history. This struggle is not between labor and the owners of the means of production but between the seed of the serpent and the seed of the woman. This brief prophecy, in the context of the curse upon the serpent, is the promise of the future.

This passage rightly has been called the protoevangelion, the protogospel. Here, in admittedly vague terms, is the first promise of the Messiah. The Good News, however, is not merely about Calvary. This passage is not only the protoevangelion; it is also the protoeschaton, our first hint of the destiny of history, of how the story ends.

As the end of the millennium approaches, many people feel free to look into the future and speculate not only about how history will end but about when it will end. It seems that each new year gives us one more reason to believe this will be the year. Each new dictator on the world stage is crammed into a "literal" understanding of Scripture, until the next one comes along.

The evangelical church has been infected with a powerful dose of pessimillennialism, the doctrine of the dark future. Most of the debate about the end of history centers on a cultural collapse and on how much of the resulting destruction Christians will have to suffer through. These sundry theories tend to create an image of a God who sits by passively, waiting for things to get bad enough before sending his Son down to clean house. None who espouse these theories would suggest that God is not in control, but the theories do tend to leave that impression. Is God really in control of history? And if he is in control, what role do the decisions and actions of men play? Where is history going, and how will we get there?

The Pattern of History

There is some insight in the Eastern view that history moves in circles, and that all of us, whether we study history or not, are doomed to repeat it. There are patterns in history, obvious repetitions of key themes. The movement of history, however, is not a true circle but a spiral, repeating themes that yet move forward to a grand climax.

James Jordan, in his outstanding but, sadly, out-of-print work *Through New Eyes* (Brentwood, Tenn.: Wolgemuth and Hyatt, 1988), makes a strong case for a liturgical pattern of history. The first step in the pattern is what Jordan calls the announcement. God assesses the situation on earth and makes known his plan of change. When God spoke to Noah he first gave his judgment on mankind. "And God said to Noah, 'The end of all flesh has come before Me, for the earth is filled with violence through them; and behold, I will destroy them with the earth. Make yourself an ark of gopherwood . . .'" (Gen. 6:13–14). God announces his plan to destroy the creation and at the same time to save those whom he has chosen.

Step two of the process, Jordan calls exodus. In this part of God's work in history God takes those he has called out and carries them to a new, remade place. In doing so God establishes a new world order.

Step three follows immediately after. Having brought his people to safety in new circumstances, he speaks again, this time not in judgment but in blessing. Jordan writes, "Third, once the exodus has been accomplished, God gives His Word of promise and command: He distributes the new world to His people, and gives them laws and rules to obey as they exercise dominion over it. In connection with this, God sets up a symbolic world model as His sanctuary. We shall call this stage by the word establishment" (p. 168).

In the fourth stage, God gets history moving again. He evaluates his people from time to time, applying the sanctions of the covenant, blessing with obedience, cursing with disobedience. Jordan calls this stage history and decline.

The fifth and final stage is judgment. God comes again in judgment, but as in the beginning of the cycle, his judgment always includes an announcement of his intention to create a new world, one grander and more glorious than the last.

Jordan calls this pattern "liturgical" because it reflects the reality of our worship: "We begin in sabbath [rest and peace] at the throne of God, move out into the world and work, and then return at the Lord's Day for His evaluation and blessing. All history proceeds from God's alpha, and develops into His never-ending omega" (p. 169).

Consider how this pattern is worked out in Noah's life. We have already mentioned how God made his announcement of impending judgment and his announcement of grace to Noah and his family. Next come the deluge and the "exodus" of Noah's family in the safety of God's ark. Once the waters have receded, Noah and his kin leave the ark and enter the establishment stage. God speaks again, this time with a promise: "Then the LORD said in His heart, 'I will never again curse the ground for man's sake, although the imagination of man's heart is evil from his youth; nor will I again destroy every living thing as I have done. While the earth remains, seedtime and harvest, and cold and heat, and winter and summer, and day and night shall not cease'" (Gen. 8:21–22).

In God's promise we even have a hint of why history works in a spiral motion. We often overlook the importance of this promise. God is promising not only that there will not be another worldwide flood but also that he will ensure the orderly operation of the universe. We have God's promise that the universe will function in fundamentally consistent ways. This promise is what makes science possible. Science operates principally through induction: the scientist gathers information from which he or she draws conclusions. The sun will come up tomorrow because it came up yesterday, and the day before, and the day before. The scientist then tests his or her hypothesis. The unspoken (and utterly gratuitous, outside of God's promise to Noah) assumption is that things will act in the future in like manner. How do we know that objects at rest tend to remain at rest unless acted upon by an outside object? The secular scientist says, "Because all the objects at rest we have observed stayed at rest unless or until they were acted upon by an outside object." The scientist who believes the Bible, however, inserts and speaks a valid assumption: "And because God has promised an orderly universe."

God then gives a blessing and a command: "So God blessed Noah and his sons, and said to them: 'Be fruitful and multiply, and fill the earth'" (Gen. 9:1). This command is a familiar one. It is the same command given to Adam and Eve in creation. Again we see the repeated pattern of how God works in history.

The pattern of history then proceeds into decline with the sins of Noah and Ham. Sin again increases until in chapter 11 of Genesis God comes down in judgment at Babel. He had given the command to Noah and his children to fill the earth. Instead the people rebel, gather together at the plain of Shinar, and plot their assault upon heaven. God comes to assess and gives out his judgment, and our attention turns to Abraham and God's announced plan for him. God will start again, so to speak, with Abraham and his seed.

So the pattern of history continues in the life of Abraham, then with his descendants, up to the clearest picture of exodus, Moses leading the people out of Egypt. One of the significant changes to note is that each "re-creation" is vastly superior to the last. It includes more people, from Adam and Eve, to Noah and his whole family, to the clan of Abraham, to the nation Israel, to the outermost parts of the world. It becomes increasingly clear, from the shadows of the protogospel in Genesis 3, to the early sacrifices of Noah, to the promise that Abraham would be a blessing to all the nations, to the full sacrificial system in the tabernacle, to the promise of David's eternal reign, to the glory of Solomon's temple. All of this reaches its greatest degree (thus far) in the proclamation of the gospel and will be finally and fully finished at the consumation of Christ's kingdom.

God and History

This is where it is all going, the fullness of Christ's kingdom, the end to which history is progressing. But our question is not so much where we are going but who is driving us there. These spirals are not the result of God watching his creation run amuck and intervening to restore some sort of order. Some people suggest that this is what makes God so strong, that he lets the universe go, setting aside his sovereignty, and like Superman, ducks into a cosmic phone booth, puts his power back on, and comes to the rescue, righting the mistakes we've made.

The entire process is in his hands and, more important, in his plans. There is no plan B with God. History is not like some fill-in-the-blank story, in which the story changes tracks every time a human makes a decision. God, assessing his creation at the time of Noah, was not surprised. He did not frantically search for some worthy family to save. He did not go back to his drawing board and strain his brain until the idea of a flood came upon him. He not only knew of the condition of man at the time, he not only planned that it would be such, he also made sure it was such. It was God who created all the secondary causes which brought about his goal of nearly universal moral decadence. It was God who worked in the heart of Noah such that he would be redeemed.

I like to give my congregation a simple outline of the entire Bible. It is easy to remember and helps to put particular events in Scripture, and in our lives, in perspective:

Genesis 1 and 2: creation

Genesis 3: fall

Genesis 4 to Revelation 22: getting back to Genesis 2, only better

That is what history is all about, the outworking of the covenant of redemption.

Presbyterians, of which I am one, love to speak about covenants. Jordan's framework of history is a covenantal framework. We speak of God's covenants with Adam, Noah, Abraham, and David and then the new covenant in the New Testament. All such covenants, while of great importance, are rooted in a covenant made before the writing of Scripture. The covenant of redemption is not the gospel, nor any covenant between God and man. Rather it is a covenant between the members of the Trinity. It is the agreement among the members of the Trinity regarding what each will do in the drama of our redemption. The Father chooses the elect. The Son secures atonement for the elect through his perfect life and death. The Spirit quickens the hearts of the elect and works with the elect for their sanctification. All of history is God working out that very plan.

Sometimes when we turn on the television news, if something of great import is happening, we are told we are watching "history in the making." Sometimes Christians get excited when we get to participate in "making history." The reality, however, is that we are not bit players on the stage of history. The spotlight is not on dictators and wars, not on droughts and earthquakes. All of these events happen not around the body of Christ but for the body of Christ. All the turmoil around the globe exists for the purpose of God working out his plan for his people. The spotlight is really always on us, because all things are done for us. We are the reason for history, though, of course, God's glory is the ultimate reason. The lights shine upon us so we may better see the God who is working all things for his glory, so we might worship him and adore him. When a covenant child is baptized, we are watching history in the making. When Moses tended his sheep for forty years, that was history in the making.

Marx was right about one thing. The end for which all of history works is indeed a paradise. It is not, however, a workers' paradise but a paradise prepared for those who recognize that their works are as filthy rags, who depend upon the work of another. Abraham was promised that his descendants would be as the dust on the ground. God was telling Abraham not only how many there would be but also where they would be. We will cover the earth, the new earth that is the last and eternal chapter of history.

We stand on the last spiral of history, waiting to enter eternity. But we stand in the second most glorious epoch, knowing so much more than Adam or Noah or David. Because, in this chapter of God's history, God has seen fit to give us the script for the last and lasting chapter. We, unlike Marx, do indeed know the future. We win, because God wins.

God the great Creator of all things
doth uphold, direct, dispose,
and govern all creatures, actions,
and things, from the greatest
even to the least. . . .

Westminster Confession of Faith,
chapter 5, section 1

WHO'S THE BOSS?

Almighty over the Mighty

All across the globe and across the span of time, wars have been waged in the thirst for power. Power is the name of the game in government. From the perspective of those who rule, the more power the better. But the founding fathers who gathered to craft and ratify America's Constitution seemed to have a very different goal in mind.

Anyone who has done even a cursory study of the Constitution or has sat through interminable lectures in Coach So-and-So's civics class knows that these United States have something unusual—a government with a system of checks and balances. Each of the three branches of the federal government has not only a job to do but an important role to play in limiting the power of the other two branches. And it doesn't stop there. The Tenth Amendment, more than anything else in the Constitution, restrains the power of the federal government. It says, essentially, "If something is not listed here in the job description of the federal government, the government must stay out. It is up to the states and the people to decide."

The signers of the Constitution were well aware of the wise warning of Lord Acton: "Power corrupts, and absolute power corrupts absolutely."

Government has been about power ever since God established it. When God gave his blessing and command to Noah after the flood, he also gave this law: "Whoever sheds man's blood, by man his blood shall be shed; for in the image of God He made man" (Gen. 9:6). Here, for the first time in the course of human events, God instituted government. Here God granted to men what some call "the power of the sword" (see Romans 13). It is an awesome power, the power of life and death. And long before Lord Acton came along to make his observation, it was a dangerous power.

As with all gifts God gives to men, men have tended to distort this power and use it for man's glory. It is not unusual for governments to persecute those they have been called to protect. Nor is it a new thing. Nor is it at all unusual for those God has placed in power to rebel against God himself. Scripture gives us a picture of that rebellion in Psalm 2: "Why do the nations rage, and the people plot a vain thing? The kings of the earth set themselves, and the rulers take counsel together, against the Lord and against His Anointed . . ." (vv. 1–2). It is in times of such persecution that the people of God are tempted to believe God is not mightier than the mighty.

Which raises the important question, Did God, in granting the power of the sword, make the mistake of giving men too much power? Or to put it another way, Is God mightier than the mighty?

God and Mighty Nations

One of God's own prophets raised this question. The prophet Habakkuk is probably best remembered for the expression "The just shall live by his faith" (2:4), which Paul used in Romans to explain the gospel. But the prophet did not begin so well. The book which bears his name begins with a lament, a complaint against God, who had allowed his people to fall into disobedience under the reign of Jehoiakim. Habakkuk begins, "O LORD, how long shall I cry, and You will not hear? even cry out to You, 'Violence!' and You will not save. Why do You show me iniquity, and cause me to see trouble? For plundering and violence are before me; there is strife, and contention arises. Therefore the law is powerless, and justice never goes forth. For the wicked surround the righteous; therefore perverse judgment proceeds" (1:2–4).

Habakkuk wasn't shy. God didn't have to ask him to stop beating around the bush. The concern here is, in large part, unjust government. The Hebrew word translated in this passage as *powerless* means, literally, "numb." In the face of unjust government, the law is ineffective.

God gave Habakkuk a rather surprising answer: "Look among the nations and watch—be utterly astounded! For I will work a work in your days which you would not believe, though it were told you" (1:5). By this time Habakkuk was both relieved and probably busy patting himself on the back for bringing to

God's attention the injustices being done in Judah. Finally, he probably thought, God will get after those bad guys.

But the surprise was still to come: "For indeed I am raising up the Chaldeans, a bitter and hasty nation which marches through the breadth of the earth, to possess dwelling places that are not theirs. They are terrible and dreadful; their judgment and their dignity proceed from themselves. Their horses also are swifter than leopards, and more fierce than evening wolves" (vv. 6–8).

Habakkuk must have thought, "The Chaldeans!?" He probably didn't need God's graphic description of their fearsomeness. Everybody was talking about the Chaldeans, the new bully on the block. But no one was talking about them the way God talked about them. Notice God did not say, "Habakkuk, don't worry about it. Luckily it so happens the Chaldeans are looking pretty strong. They'll probably get to Judah sooner or later, and they'll probably do something to alleviate the situation of which you complained."

This nation that God described so vividly as rapacious, vicious, and guilty of all manner of evil is the same nation God said he was raising up. The destruction which the Chaldeans would soon bring to bear upon Judah is the "work" God promised he would do. God is not only mightier than the mighty; he is the very source of their might.

Habakkuk, who began by complaining about the wickedness in his own government, who focused on what appeared to be God's inability to control one wayward government, found out that God's solution was an even viler government.

Was Habakkuk satisfied? Did he understand the peace that comes from knowing God controls even the most evil oppressors? Did he respond with a sigh of relief to God's promise that all was very much under his control? Not Habakkuk, who seemed to be happy only when he was unhappy. He raised yet another lament, that God would allow such a juggernaut to assault the very Judah he had first complained about. He not only lamented but also issued a challenge to God: "I will stand my watch and set myself on the rampart, and watch to see what He will say to me . . ." (2:1).

But Habakkuk was learning. The God he worshiped is not only all powerful but all knowing. Habakkuk knew he wouldn't stump God, for he added, "And what I will answer when I am reproved" (2:1). God did indeed answer and made judgment upon the very nation he raised up as a scourge: "Indeed, because he transgresses by wine, he is a proud man, and he does not stay at home. Because he enlarges his desire as hell, and he is like death, and cannot be satisfied, he gathers to himself all nations and heaps up for himself all peoples" (2:5).

God's response did not stop with his assessment of the Chaldeans but continued with his plans for them: "Shall not all these take up a proverb against him, and a taunting riddle against him, and say, 'Woe to him who increases what is not his—how long? and to him who loads himself up with many pledges? Will not your creditors rise up suddenly? Will they not awaken and oppress you? And you will become their booty. Because you have plundered many nations, all the remnant of the people shall plunder you . . .'" (2:6–8).

"Habakkuk," God was saying, "don't worry about the wickedness of the Chaldeans. I've got plans for them. The empire will not hold for its very size." God had raised up wicked rulers in Judah for the sake of his people. He had raised up a wicked empire in the

Chaldeans for the sake of the rulers. And he would raise up a remnant among the conquered to destroy the Chaldeans.

There was no part of the equation outside God's sovereign control. Habakkuk should have known that. This was not the first time in history (nor the last) that God used the powerful for his own purposes.

God and Mighty Rulers

In Israel's birth we have another such story. Exodus begins with a brief account of how the children of Abraham had come to Egypt. Then verse 8 of the first chapter gives us this ominous warning: "Now there arose a new king over Egypt, who did not know Joseph." God had blessed Jacob's family such that they had grown great in number. And their growth had put fear into Pharaoh. His response was threefold. First, he subjected the Hebrews to slavery. Second, he instructed the Hebrew midwives to kill the sons and spare the daughters. Third, when that failed, he ordered that all firstborn male Hebrew babies be thrown into the river. That is vile and powerful government.

You know how the story goes. God sent Moses to tell Pharaoh to "let my people go." But God warned Moses from the beginning that it would take great signs and wonders to bend the will of the Pharaoh. Indeed, God promised his prophet Moses that he would harden the heart of Pharaoh. We will discuss that promise more in a later chapter. What is important here is God's connection to Pharaoh's power. God always has his purposes, and sometimes he tells us those purposes: "Then the LORD said to Moses, 'Rise early in the morning and stand before Pharaoh, and say to him, "Thus says the LORD God of the Hebrews: 'Let My people go, that they may serve Me, for at this time I will send all My plagues to your very heart, and on your servants and on your people, that you may know that there is none like Me in all the earth'"'" (Exod. 9:13–14). God let Pharaoh know he was not dealing with another petty deity. God willed to show his strength, in part, so Pharaoh would recognize God and his might.

But God had not merely entered into a contest. He hadn't strutted onto Pharaoh's stage to flex his divine muscles: "Now if I had stretched out My hand and struck you and your people with pestilence, then you would have been cut off from the earth. But indeed for this purpose I have raised you up, that I may show My power in you, and that My name might be declared in all the earth" (vv. 15–16).

God, through Moses, announced to Pharaoh three critical truths. First, God could wipe Pharaoh and all those with him from the face of the earth, if he so desired. Second, Pharaoh's power was not merely tolerated by God, but God was the one who gave it to him. "I raised you up." It's like an episode of the *Twilight Zone*. Pharaoh had gone through his life impressed with his power, self-absorbed, believing himself to be both center-stage and self-made. It seems corruption is not the only necessary corollary of power; pride is too. But suddenly a messenger from the real playwright came on stage and explained what Pharaoh's role was in this drama. And judging from the proof the messenger brought, it was not such a great role after all. Third, all of Pharaoh's life, his power, his pomp, had come about just so the God of this raggedy old shepherd could make a name for himself.

In the pivotal moment of the New Testament, we are given a glimpse of another confused ruler who knew not from whence came his power. To be sure, Pontius Pilate did not have the same measure of power as Pharaoh. He had human authorities to answer to in Rome. The evidence seems to suggest Pilate wasn't the most forceful leader on the world stage at the time. Nevertheless, he, like Pharaoh, recognized a threat when he saw one.

First he tried to skirt the issue of what to do about Jesus. When the chief priests refused to dirty their hands by executing Jesus, Pilate began his interrogation, "Are You the King of the Jews?" (John 18: 33). Jesus hardly responded with the respect to which Pilate had become accustomed: "Are you speaking for yourself on this, or did others tell you this about Me?" (v. 34). Pilate asked a second time, "Are You a king then?" (v. 37). Jesus answered enigmatically, "You say rightly that I am a king. For this cause I was born, and for this cause I have come into the world, that I should bear witness to the truth. Everyone who is of the truth hears My voice" (v. 37). Pilate, either cynically or burdened with uncertainty, asked, "What is truth?"

Pilate must have been frustrated. He was used to grovelling prisoners, not those that stand with dignity before his majesty. Perhaps fearing that Jesus wasn't altogether sane, Pilate informed him of the gravity of the proceedings: "'Do You not know that I have the power to crucify You, and power to release You?' Jesus answered, 'You could have no power at all against Me unless it had been given you from above. Therefore the one who delivered Me to you has the greater sin'" (19:10–11).

Again not only did God have more power than Pilate but he was the very source of any power Pilate had.

And we are not talking about something as comparatively petty as a marauding army conquering the known world; here we have a man about to put the Son of Man to death. God is mightier than the mighty because all might is his.

Ruler of the Rulers

We sometimes experience feelings of powerlessness. We alternately beat our heads against the walls of justice and shrug and confess with the world, "You can't fight City Hall." We are frustrated that those who rule over us seem to turn a deaf ear to our pleas for justice. And so we often wonder if anyone rules those who rule us. The Bible, however, is abundantly clear that he who is all justice rules over those who won't practice justice. Elections come and go. Coups and revolts come and go. Legislative sessions come and go. We watch news reports with bated breath, waiting and wondering. We send our letters and make our phone calls, pleading with our representatives to obey God's commands. We fret and we worry as election results trickle in. We grumble like Habakkuk at the throne of God. We forget that whether it is the Chaldeans or the Clintonians, whether it is the governor of Judea or the governor of our own state, none is mightier than the Mighty One.

Because God is unchangeably enthroned in heaven, because his kingdom encompasses all of creation, and because all rulers are his ministers, empowered by him, we can say with assurance that through it all, our God reigns.

*Although, in relation to
the foreknowledge and decree
of God, the first Cause, all things
come to pass immutably,
and infallibly; yet, by the same
providence, he ordereth them to fall
out, according to the nature
of second causes, either necessarily,
freely, or contingently.*

Westminster Confession of Faith,
chapter 5, section 2

6

WHO'S MINDING THE STORE?

Almighty over the Details

Many people are comforted by the knowledge of God's sovereignty over the great events. Our sensibilities are not terribly disturbed by God's control over kings and potentates. It is seemly for God to govern the affairs of the powerful and influential. It is not our habit to dine at the White House or to serve drinks to the Pharaoh of Egypt. It's God's business to direct the great men of history. He is great and we are small.

But what about the details of our everyday lives? Isn't God too busy watching over North and South Korea to be concerned with my daily commute to the office or factory? Even my boss is not looking over my shoulder to make sure every *i* is dotted or every widget arranged just right. My boss is paid to look at the big picture. We don't think much of powerful people who meddle in our comparatively mundane lives. We see such meddling as a sign of insecurity and a lack of trust. Surely God is far too grand and glorious a being to be concerned with the details, isn't he?

Big Events and Small Details

The creation account doesn't give a great many details, and therein lies a problem. Nothing gets a tired conversation started like arguing over creation. Were they six literal days, or is the Hebrew *yom* merely a figure of speech? Couldn't God have created conditions such that evolution would work, and then stepped back to watch his plan come to pass? I won't argue this issue here, but I will note that when the Bible teaches about God's creation of light, all it says is, "And there was light." It doesn't explain how or why light came to have some of its strange properties, sometimes acting like a wave and other times acting like a particle. Albert Einstein claimed that as things approach the speed of light, they approach infinite mass. Thankfully, he was wrong. If light took on infinite mass as it not only approaches but reaches the speed of light, we'd all have a serious headache every time we turned a light on. Forget eye strain; we'd all be pancakes after getting hit by infinite mass.

Light, of course, is not the only mystery that still eludes the probing minds of scientists. When I was studying chemistry, my teachers laughed at the antiquated notions they were taught about the nature of matter. Then they would proceed to drill into our young and trusting minds that protons, neutrons, and electrons are the smallest bits of matter. And I believed them. Until I read about quarks and subquarks—even smaller bits of matter. Expect any day now for scientists to announce that subquarks are made up of something called sub-subquarks. It is a small world after all.

Einstein wasn't always wrong. When some of his colleagues argued that some of these tiny bits of matter move in a random fashion, Einstein quipped, "God doesn't play dice." There Einstein showed wisdom. There Einstein recognized what, or rather who, is at the long end of causal chains in science's pursuit of ultimates. Why do two hydrogen molecules join with an oxygen molecule to make water? We are told it's because of the number of electrons in each and the nature of their orbits. Why do they orbit the way they do? I don't know, but I presume it has something to do with sub-subatomic particles.

Real scientists probably could continue to explain several more levels of questions. Eventually, however, they will hit a wall. Eventually they will have to say either, "For no reason," or with Einstein, "Because God wills it so."

God is not only strong enough to control the mighty; he also controls the tiny. And when you consider the size of the universe, and the size of sub-sub- and probably sub some more atomic particles, that's a very large number of tinies.

With God there are no contingencies, events which are possible but are not certain to happen. When I flip a coin in the air, from my perspective the outcome is a contingency. I can only conclude that barring the coin landing on its side, it will come up either heads or tails. But is it a matter of chance? What determines whether the coin will come up heads or tails? The variables are staggering. The barometric pressure, the pressure applied by my thumb, whether and how high I catch the coin, whether I do the last-second flip after catching the coin, the weight and density of the coin, whether the coin started with heads up or tails—all these are proximate causes, the chain of causes bringing about a heads or tails result. Then we have another layer of proximate causes to explore. How did the barometric pressure get to be what it was? Why did I flip with a particular force? Answering these how and why questions keeps us going back farther and farther into more and more layers of variables. Along the way we probably will be tempted to shrug our shoulders and answer, "Just because." We mean one of two things with this penetrating response. Sometimes we mean, "There is a reason for this, a cause I do not know and am unable to find out." That's fine. God has neither made us omniscient nor commanded us to be so. But sometimes we mean, "There is no reason or cause." That is a problem.

As we discussed earlier, every effect must have a sufficient cause. There are no spontaneous events; no effects without causes. And because every effect has a cause, there are no contingencies as far as God is concerned. He knows the barometric pressure. He also knows why that pressure is what it is. He knows the weight of the coin and the strength of my thumb muscle. There is no part of the equation God doesn't understand, no event of which he must ask, "I wonder which way it will go?" There are no unaccounted for causes out there, no causes of which he is not the ultimate cause.

The truth is that even God could not control the big events of history if he did not also control the smallest details. We all know the little ditty that reminds us there really is no line between the big and the small: "For want of a nail, the shoe was lost. For want of the shoe, the horse was lost. For want of the horse, the rider was lost. For want of the rider, the battle was lost. For want of the battle, the war was lost." Imagine the wonder in this truth. One nation conquered by another all because of a few ounces of metal.

One theologian friend of mine has said that the universe cannot contain both a sovereign God and "one maverick molecule," one small speck outside of God's control. He then goes a step further, explaining that the universe could not contain any god and a maverick molecule. That one maverick molecule could be the very one that holds the nail, and thus the shoe and the rider, in place. Whatever God does not control is stronger than God, and thus becomes god.

But the Bible, while affirming that nature itself communicates God's sovereign control over all things (Rom. 1:20), gives us in the clearer light of special revelation the same information. Perhaps no biblical story better illustrates God's control over the tiniest details than the story of Ruth.

Ruth

You remember Ruth's circumstance. Facing famine in Judah, Elimelech, his wife, Naomi, and their two sons emigrated to Moab. After Elimelech died, one son married Ruth, a Moabitess. The other son married Orpah. Ten years passed and both sons died. Naomi, in God's providence, was without a husband or sons to care for her. Remembering how widows were cared for in her native Israel, Naomi decided to return home, and encouraged her daughters-in-law to stay and seek new husbands. Orpah found wisdom in the counsel, but Ruth responded differently: "Entreat me not to leave you, or to turn back from following after you; for wherever you go, I will go; and wherever you lodge, I will lodge; your people shall be my people, and your God, my God" (Ruth 1:16). And so the two women journeyed to Israel. In verse 19 we are told, "And it happened, when they had come to Bethlehem, that all the city was excited because of them." The phrase "and it happened" crops up again and again in the narrative. They arrived at the beginning of the barley harvest, and Ruth was allowed to glean in the fields of Boaz, one of Naomi's relatives.

In chapter 3 we are told that after the barley and wheat harvests were finished, Naomi said to Ruth, "My daughter, should I not try to find a home for you, where you will be well provided for? Is not Boaz, with whose servant girls you have been, a kinsman of ours?" (NIV). And she told Ruth to go to him that night and follow certain instructions. So Ruth went to see Boaz while he was sleeping. "Now it happened at midnight that the man was startled, and turned himself; and there, a woman was lying at his feet" (3:8).

As a result of this meeting, Ruth and Boaz were later married. And by God's grace they conceived and Ruth gave birth to a son, Obed. Obed, of course, married and fathered a son, Jesse. Jesse also married and had children. One of them became King David, to whom God promised an everlasting kingdom, a kingdom consummated by Jesus.

We can look at this story in the same light as the ditty about the war. For want of rain, there was a famine. For want of food, Elimelech and Naomi moved to Moab. For want of Jewish women to marry, Elimelech's son married Ruth. Later, for want of husbands, the ladies trekked back to Israel. For want of food, Ruth gleaned in Boaz's fields. For want of sleep, Boaz determined to marry Ruth. Because of the marriage, we have, in turn, Obed, Jesse, David, even Jesus himself.

And all the "for want ofs" are not just fortuitous circumstances. It's not as though God woke up one day and much to his surprise found a drought in the land. It's not as though God saw Elimelech die and worried, "Now what will I do for poor Naomi?" All the circumstances which preceeded the birth of David were in God's holy hands. They look like small details, but they were not. There are no small details.

Allow me to make a caveat here. Those who rejoice in God's sovereignty, those who are ready to say, "Yes, God did this," face a temptation. It is a short but dangerous step from saying "God did this" to "God did this because . . ." We do know two ultimate reasons why God does what he does: All things happen (1) because they glorify God and (2) because they are good for his people. But how they glorify God and aid his people is usually not revealed. I once read a sermon by a Puritan pastor that powerfully illustrates the temptation. If any group of people affirmed God's sovereignty, it was the Puritans. But this sermon was built not on the special revelation of Scripture but on a sloppy interpretation of nature. It seems this pastor had discovered a copy of the Church of England's Book of Common Prayer. That work was one of the very things the Puritans wanted to purify out of the church. They were not fans. But the pastor saw that this particular copy had been rather heavily chewed on by a little church mouse. Now, was this an insignificant detail? I agree with the Puritans that God did, by the most holy counsel of his will, ordain that that particular mouse would eat that particular book at that particular time. But the pastor concluded from God's ordaining this thing that God was communicating his divine displeasure at the Book of Common Prayer. Had I been there I believe I would have offered the pastor an alternate interpretation of the event. What if God actually had been saying, "The Book of Common Prayer is so wonderful that even my creature the mouse knows to feed upon it"? It could go either way, couldn't it? There could be innumerable understandings about this historical event. Beware of trying to read God's mind. It is enough to know the two ultimate reasons for all that he does.

But have I made this mistake with the story of Ruth? Is her story enough for us to conclude that God is sovereign over the details? The Book of Ruth is a historical narrative. One of the fundamentals of sound biblical interpretation is that we interpret the events of history in the Bible in light of the didactic parts of the Bible, the parts meant to present teachings. We do not look at the life of Solomon and conclude that since Solomon had many wives, it is a good thing to take many wives. Rather we look to the teachings in the first two chapters of Genesis and to the teachings of Jesus and Paul for our understanding of marriage.

Thankfully, we have more to go on than just the story of Ruth. Jesus himself spoke on the subject of God's control over the details. Jesus was about to send the disciples out to preach the kingdom, heal the sick, and cast out demons. One might expect that being called to such a ministry would bring great accolades. Wouldn't you cheer for a genuine healer? But Jesus warned his disciples of what they could expect: "And you will be hated by all for My name's sake" (Matt. 10:22). Not a very encouraging thought. Jesus warned that they would be persecuted and brought before kings and councils, and that they, like their master, would be considered by many to be agents of the devil. Jesus didn't warn them not to fear; rather he warned them of whom they should fear: "Whatever I tell you in the dark, speak in the light; and what you hear in the ear, preach on the housetops. And do not fear those who kill the body but cannot kill the soul. But rather fear Him who is able to destroy both soul and body in hell" (10:27–28). There is no typo in that last sentence. "Him" is capitalized because it refers to the Father. They were to fear their Father in heaven, whom they could not even see, but not to fear those men who actually threatened their lives. But, interestingly, right after Jesus directed the attention of the disciples toward the true object of their fear, he also reminded them that this same Father was also the source of their comfort: "Are not two sparrows sold for a copper coin? And not one of them falls to the ground apart from your Father's will. But the very hairs of your head are all numbered. Do not fear therefore: you are of more value than many sparrows" (10:29–31).

Note he didn't promise that nothing uncomfortable would befall them. Among Jesus' hearers were John, who would later be exiled to Patmos, and Peter, who would one day be crucified upside down. Too many people look at the suffering of those who call upon Christ's name and conclude either that God can't stop it or that he is unfair because he won't. We will deal more closely with suffering in a later chapter.

*God hath endued the will of man
with that natural liberty, that it
is neither forced, nor, by any absolute
necessity of nature, determined. . . .*

Westminster Confession of Faith,
chapter 9, section 1

7

Who's Choosing Whom?

Almighty over Men

There might be some readers who don't find God's sovereignty over the details too terribly comforting. Some, I would bet, are squirming. Probably some got so distressed over the idea that God ordained when they would put this book down that they did so, vowing never to pick it up again, perhaps even in a vain attempt to thwart the plan of almighty God. And perhaps you are saying in the privacy of your mind, "But if God is sovereign over every detail of our lives, then we are all nothing but puppets!"

Does God's absolute control over every event, human and otherwise, make us mere puppets? The argument that such control robs us of our dignity and makes us subhuman is common. It is not, however, sound. In the first place it is not an argument. Rather, it is a statement of preference. To make it an argument, one must add the two unspoken premises it operates under. The first is this: We don't want to be puppets. The second is: We don't have to be anything we don't want to be. This second premise is false. God has not said we need not be anything we don't want to be.

Before we answer the charge, we need to recognize that it doesn't really matter. The issue of free will and divine sovereignty is not merely over who, man or God, will have control. It is also over who will have more dignity. If our choices are to diminish the majesty of man or to diminish the majesty of God, well, there really is no choice, is there? There is, however, a *tertium quid,* a third option. It may just be that man is not a puppet and God is still sovereign.

Causes and Compulsions

A more sophisticated version of the "argument" is to call any position which affirms God's absolute control over all things "fatalism." Some commit the "poisoning the well" fallacy, whereby you do not refute a position but instead merely associate it with an unpleasant position. Some say the Reformed doctrine of the sovereignty of God is the same as the Muslim position, which creates necessarily a deadly passiveness because "Allah wills it."

Is there a distinction? I believe there is, and it is rooted in the difference between primary and secondary causes and between internal and external compulsion. Let's go back to the story of Ruth to see how this works. There are a host of ways to answer the question, Why did Ruth marry Boaz? You can look at the primary cause: Because God willed it from before all time. Or you can look at a whole slew of secondary causes:

Because she wanted to marry Boaz.
Because she was a widow in need of a husband.
Because her husband had died.
Because she loved Naomi and wanted to follow her.
Because there was a famine in Judah.
Because Boaz happened to wake up.

All of these secondary causes were real, active. They made a difference in how the story proceeded. If Ruth's husband had lived, she would have stayed married to him, probably living her whole life in Moab and never meeting Boaz. If there had been no famine in Judah, Elimelech and Naomi wouldn't have moved to Moab, and Ruth wouldn't have married Naomi's son and eventually gone to Judah with Naomi. All of these secondary causes were part of God's plan. It was because God ordained even the details that things worked out the way they did. God did not merely write into his plan of history, "Ruth and Boaz get married." Ruth was not minding her own business in Moab when she suddenly found herself in Boaz's home. We must remember that God ordains the means as well as the ends. He planned every detail along the way.

Here is where Islam errs. Stories are told of extreme Muslims who sit back passively while their children die of some illness. When asked why they do not seek medical attention, they reply, "If Allah wills that the child should live, he will live." Of course, Allah doesn't will anything, because Allah is not. But if he were, and if he were a sovereign god, isn't it possible that he wills the child should live by means of the parents pursuing medical attention?

By the way, if the child does die, it is because, ultimately, Yahweh willed it by means of the ignorance of the parents, who do not or will not understand means and ends.

It is only when we forget that God's sovereignty includes his means that we fall into such trouble. God determines or ordains not only what will happen but also how it will happen. And we fall into the trouble when we fail to remember that one of the means God sovereignly uses is our own desires. Several of the secondary causes we listed that brought Boaz and Ruth together include things clearly outside the control of the various people involved. Naomi did not choose to be born in Judah. Nobody on earth plotted and planned a famine in the land. But there are several other secondary causes that had a great deal to do with the wishes of those involved. Elimelech, though he did not choose for the famine to come, did choose to deal with the situation by going to Moab. God did not grab him by the ear and drag him off to Moab. Elimelech looked at his circumstance and made a decision. Ruth and her first husband probably had some desire to marry one another. Certainly when Naomi announced her plans to go back to Judah, Ruth had a choice. That choice is amply illustrated by the choice of Orpah.

What if Orpah had given Naomi the moving speech Ruth gave and if Ruth had gone in search of a new

Moabite husband? We don't know what would have happened. It could be that the Book of Orpah would follow Judges in our Bibles. Or it could be that Boaz would have decided to go to Moab for some reason. The truth is that it could not have gone any other way. It was necessary that it would happen exactly the way it happened. So did God force Ruth to go with Naomi, and Orpah to stay behind? By no means. Ruth meant what she said to Naomi. She wanted to go, and at the same time, God had ordained that she would go. God had ordained that one of the means by which David would be born would be Ruth's sincere desire to stay with Naomi wherever she went.

This is what we mean when we make a distinction between internal and external compulsion. To say that Ruth was forced to go with Naomi usually means that someone or something compelled her, drove her against her will. But we can say she was forced if we mean that she had to go.

Why did she have to go? Because she wanted to go. The compulsion was internal. As we discussed in chapter 3, we always choose according to our strongest inclination at a given moment. If someone had offered Ruth the choice of staying with her first husband and Naomi in Moab instead of losing her husband and her father-in-law and going to Judah, perhaps she would have desired that choice.

But it doesn't work that way. She wasn't given that choice. Despite what the television and the self-esteem mongers claim, we cannot do whatever we want. I have two very strange daydreams. The first is to be a minor-league shortstop. There is less pressure, less hype in the minor leagues. And you can make a living playing baseball. The second daydream is to be a left-footed kicker in the NFL. There's plenty of pressure and lots of excitement there, but not much chance of getting hurt. But these will always be only daydreams. I'm too small, slow, and clumsy to have anyone pay me to play shortstop, and I can't hit a curveball. I'm too old, weak, and clumsy to be a kicker, and I'm right-footed. These are not choices I've made. I never asked to be small and slow. So God has, through circumstances that are very much within his control (it would not have been hard for him to make me big and fast and left footed), limited my choices.

But I also will never be a mathematician. And it has little to do with natural talents. I always managed to score fairly well in standardized math scores. Despite the skills I have (if I haven't lost them), I know I won't be a mathematician because I don't much care for math. I have chosen other than math for a vocation.

In neither circumstance could one rightly say I have been forced out of a profession. There are no minor-league scouts telling me that though I have just the tools they're looking for, they won't let me play, "Just because." Neither do I reject math because of an external force. No one is saying I cannot be a mathematician. But in another sense, I am forced. My wife might say, "Look, there's a lot more money to be made in math. The hours are better, and nobody gets raging mad at you because of your 'view' in math." And I might think that though there are many appealing elements about being a mathematician, the math part I don't like. I didn't choose not to like math. I can't say to myself, "Think of all that money, and stop disliking math," any more than I can tell myself, "Think about being thin and start liking green beans more than you like french fries."

Puppets and Clay

This is why the puppet analogy breaks down. First, the puppet, except for Pinocchio, doesn't have self-conciousness. Even a puppet aware of its condition as a puppet would have more dignity than one with no awareness at all (though it would also be more sad). Second, with the puppet there is no connection between the action of the puppet and the wish of the puppet. A self-conscious puppet doesn't dance proximately because it wants to dance. It dances only and ulimately because the puppet master wants it to dance. Our choices are indeed ultimately in God's sovereign control. Yet proximately we do what we do because we want to.

And one thing puppets never do is complain to the puppet master. They probably would complain if they were able. The puppet master has no feelings toward the puppet. He makes the puppet dance for his own profit. He keeps the puppet in a box. He also makes mistakes, tangling the strings and messing up the story. We, on the other hand, grumble.

A better analogy than a puppet and puppet master is given in the Bible. We are clay, and God is the potter. But God is no ordinary potter. His control over us, the way he shapes us, always serves and serves perfectly two fundamental goals. The first is that all men are what they are and do what they do ultimately for the glory of the Potter.

This is not only a legitimate goal; it is also the only legitimate ultimate goal.

This too is difficult for us. We are told time and again in Scripture to think more highly of others than ourselves. We are told to seek the well-being of others. We are told not to seek our own glory. Does God have a double standard? Some say it would be a sin for God to go about seeking his own glory. And because God cannot sin, he cannot be motivated by the desire of his own glory.

The problem with this line of reasoning is twofold. First, it fails to recognize the signficant differences between the creature and the creator. There are all kinds of things God may do consistent with his holy character that men may not do. We have different offices, different roles. We understand the role distinction in the human sphere. It would be wrong for me, for instance, to put a man in an electric chair and kill him. That doesn't mean it is always wrong for the state to do such things. The state has been given the power of the sword. It has been ordained by God to be his minister of justice. I have not; rather I have been ordained as a minister of the gospel.

In like manner, God has a different role than we do. We are not to seek after our own glory precisely because it is his glory which we are to seek. We are not to serve ourselves, because he alone is worthy of our service. To suggest that God may not seek his own glory is akin to suggesting that because God forbids us to worship other gods, we may not worship him. We make the mistake of trying to mold God in our image when we try to make him be anything other than consumed with his glory.

Second, this line of reasoning has no basis in Scripture. God is very clear in his Word that it is his glory that he is pursuing. Paul, you'll remember, when discussing God's sovereignty was quick to warn the church at Rome that God is above our judgments, that the clay ought not complain to the Potter. In Romans 11 he discusses part of why this is so in this pregnant, brief doxology: "For who has known the mind of the LORD? Or who has become His counselor? Or who has first given to Him and it shall be repaid to him? For of Him and through Him and to Him are all things, to whom be glory forever" (vv. 34–36). We are comfortable with the notion that all things are of him and through him. He is not only our creator but our sustainer. But what can it mean that all things are "to him"? It means that all things—not a few, not some, not most, but all—are for him. Their single goal is his glory, the same glory that Paul prays for forever.

Paul was not teaching some new doctrine. He was familiar with Isaiah, through whom God spoke, saying, "Remember the former things of old, for I am God, and there is no other; I am God, and there is none like Me, declaring the end from the beginning, and from ancient times things that are not yet done, saying, 'My counsel shall stand, and I will do all My pleasure'" (Isa. 46:9–10). God does all his pleasure. And his pleasure is his glory.

We are not puppets. We are human beings, made in the image of God. We make real choices, according to our desires. To be sure, our choices are never ultimate causes, yet they are real causes. And all those choices, one way or another, are his pleasure as well.

That brings us to the second fundamental goal of the Potter: the well-being of his elect. If we are not one of his children, we can rest in the knowledge that even the dread which awaits us in hell is still his pleasure and will glorify him. But if we are his, we also know that it is his pleasure first that we glorify him through his redeeming us, and second that everything he has planned in our lives works for our good.

God's ways are not our ways. He has not revealed to us exactly how he is glorified in all that takes place. Neither has he revealed to us how all the hardships we face work together for our good. We don't have to know. The hows are some of the "things not seen" which make up the meaning of faith. Faith is believing God. We are, like children, to believe what he chooses to reveal, without insisting he reveal all things to us. In fact, in those many circumstances in which we can see neither how he is glorified nor how the circumstances work toward our good, even that ignorance glorifies him and is good for those that are his.

God, in his ordinary providence, maketh use of means, yet is free to work without, above, and against them, at his pleasure.

Westminster Confession of Faith,
chapter 5, section 3

8

WHO REIGNS?

Almighty over the Devil

The devil is a clever being, the craftiest of the beasts. C. S. Lewis highlights some of that craftiness in one of his great works, *The Screwtape Letters*. The book is a series of letters from a senior demon, Screwtape, to a demon apprentice, Wormwood. Wormwood is given the task of working on his "patient," a human he is trying to lead astray. The greatness of the book is in how Lewis sees through the devil's cleverness.

Screwtape, very early on, highlights the broader strategy of his "father below." He notes that the devil usually takes one of two approaches. In some times and in some places, the devil wants people to be preoccupied with him, to fear him, to be fascinated by him. Then the devil is able to work his will through fear and enticement.

In other circumstances, however, the devil prefers to operate behind the scenes. Rather than wanting people to fear him, he wants them to forget him or to disbelieve in him. He knows that what we don't know can hurt us. For the last hundred years or so in America, the devil has practiced this strategy. He chooses wisely and reacts to the strategies of the church.

Consider our image of the devil. Have you ever wondered how the devil came to be pictured wearing red tights and carrying a pitchfork? It was a strategy of the medieval church. The church recognized that the devil's great sin is pride. That is what matters most to him. Thus, they reasoned, the best way to get him is to mock him, to attack his pride by presenting him as a comical character. This strategy, of course, was born in a time when the devil was thought to be very real. The church of the Middle Ages is to be commended at least for having attempted to thwart the devil. That same caricature that attacked his pride, however, came to be very useful for the devil's strategy of hiding. Ask anyone if they believe in the devil, and that comical image springs to mind, and most respond, "Of course not." Just as he planned.

God and the Devil

Much of what has been said about how strong God is rests upon the fundamental idea that God is the Creator. He is *sui generis,* in a class by himself. We have been making important distinctions between the Creator and creations. The Creator is eternal, immutable, self-existent, having the power of being within himself. He is the Creator; we are not.

Within the category of created beings, however, there remain degrees of power, significance, and authority. No creature stood higher than the one they called Lucifer. He was a superior being, the supreme creature. He stood at the pinnacle of the created order. He was God's finest work. Ezekiel describes him as "the model of perfection, full of wisdom and perfect in beauty" (Ezek. 28:12).

Ezekiel's description, however, gets to the heart of the matter when in verse 15 he adds, "until iniquity was found in you." Greek tragedy trafficked in tales of how the mighty have fallen, but none can compare to the disparity between the height of Satan and the depth of his fall. How Satan fell, how one so filled with wisdom came to be consumed with pride, we will not here address. The same principles we applied to the fall of Adam in chapter 3 apply to the devil. That is to say, he could not change his own nature from good to evil. And of course, he can't blame it on the devil; he is the devil. The important thing is that he did fall. And with him fell a host of angels, now demons.

Since Satan's character changed, his goal has been the same. It is his desire to derail the plans of God. In many ways he is God's opposite. God is all good, but there is no good in the devil, only evil. God loves mankind, but the devil hates all men, even those who consciously worship him. God's abode is heaven; the devil's, hell. The perennial danger, however, is to push this comparison too far. Too many of us, especially in those times and places where the devil practices the strategy of being more open, believe in a sort of practical Manichaeism.

Manichaeism, while not a philosophy propagated by too many evangelists these days, was once a virulent heresy that attacked the Christian faith. Mani was a third-century thinker who combined Persian, Christian, and Buddhist theologies to create a whole new system of thought. The key feature of Mani's theology was dualism. He affirmed that what he called the Father of Lights and the Prince of Darkness were both eternal and independent. Neither was dependent on the other, neither created by the other. This theory essentially affirmed there are two gods, one good and the other bad. They are equal in power.

Again, you would be hard pressed to find T-shirts proclaiming the glory of this odd faith. The strange thing, however, is that many professed Christians seem to affirm this dualism. They see the devil as the "bad god." The phenomenal success of Frank Peretti's novels may have something to do with this. Peretti, in a laudable effort to communicate the importance of prayer, treated his readers to images of physical battles in the spiritual realm between angels and demons, wherein the angels fight more effectively under "prayer cover." Many readers, much to Peretti's regret, took this literary tool a little too literally. They believed that the battle between God and his hosts and the devil and his minions is somehow up in the air. (And presumably they didn't ask the obvious question: What happens to the angels and devils who lose these sword fights? Do the angels go to heaven and the demons go to hell?)

But Scripture paints no such portrait of the relationship between good and evil. There is no question anywhere in the Bible of whether God is mightier than the devil. The battle between the devil and God is first brought to our attention in Genesis 3. You remember that the serpent beguiled Eve, and the fall took place. God pronounced judgment on Adam and Eve, announcing his sanctions against his subjects for breaking covenant. But he didn't do this until after doing the same with the devil: "Because you have done this, you are cursed more than all cattle, and more than every beast of the field; on your belly you shall go, and you shall eat dust all the days of your life. And I will put enmity between you and the woman, and between your seed and her Seed; He shall bruise your head, and you shall bruise His heel" (Gen. 3:14–15). We've already seen that this is the protogospel, but it also affirms clearly that God is mightier than the devil. Notice Satan did not respond. There was no sinister, "We'll just see about that!" as he slunk off, nor a more direct, "Who do you think you are?" to the Creator. God can pronounce judgment on the serpent because he rules over him.

It is not long after this (at least in terms of time, though it is much later in Scripture) that we meet the devil again. Most scholars believe Job lived in the time of the patriarchs. The Book of Job begins with a description of Job's life and character, before quickly switching scenes to the very throne room of God.

"Now there was a day when the sons of God came to present themselves before the LORD, and Satan also came among them. And the LORD said to Satan, 'From where do you come?' So Satan answered the LORD and said, 'From going to and fro on the earth, and from walking back and forth on it.' Then the LORD said to Satan, 'Have you considered My servant Job, that there is none like him on the earth, a blameless and upright man, one who fears God and shuns evil?'" (Job 1:6–8).

Note a couple of elements of the story already. The first is that Satan came with "the sons of God." These are almost certainly angels who came into God's throne room. The devil cannot barge in on God at will. Second, and perhaps more important, note what the devil was doing. According to his own report he was "walking to and fro" on the earth. One of our common mistakes is to ascribe to the devil properties which belong to God alone. God does not wander the earth; he is omnipresent. The devil, on the other hand, can be only one place at a time. This helps me not to fear the devil so much, if only because I know it is unlikely I will ever face him. The devil is busy with men and women far more important to him than me. I'm sure he's assigned a mere buck private to me.

Satan, however much he might be under God's sovereignty, did not respond to God's question in an appropriate way: "So Satan answered the Lord and said, 'Does Job fear God for nothing? Have You not made a hedge around him, around his household, and around all that he has on every side? You have blessed the work of his hands, and his possessions have increased in the land'" (vv. 9–10). Satan challenged God's claim that Job was an upright man. He did not bow before God's sovereign authority. He did, however, recognize two key facts. The first is that God is sovereign over the accumulation of wealth. That does not mean that all upright men will be wealthy or that all poor men are wicked (as the story of Job so clearly and powerfully teaches), but it does remind us that his rule includes the making of wealth. Second, notice that Satan referred to the "hedge" God had placed around Job and his possessions. Satan cannot even get at the wealth of God, not because God will wrestle and tussle with Satan but because God can, by the mere power of his word, bar access.

The devil then made his bargain: "But now stretch out Your hand and touch all that he has, and he will surely curse You to Your face!" (v. 11). Note that Satan did not ask for permission to torment Job but asked that God do it himself. God, not the devil, is the one with the power to destroy Job and his wealth. God, however, delegated this task to the devil: "So the LORD said to Satan, 'Behold, all that he has is in your power; only do not lay a hand on his person'" (v. 12).

It is important to note that not only did the devil have to get permission to torment Job, he didn't even have the power to do so unless God granted him that power. It's not as though all that happened is the devil asked, "May I go and torment Job?" He also had to ask, "May I have the necessary power to do that? Would you grant me that power?"

Of course, the devil wouldn't even have the power to exist if God had not given him that power. Like all creatures, the devil is dependent upon God for his very existence. God is sustaining the devil every second he exists. If the Father wished that the devil were no longer to exist, it wouldn't take any strain on him to accomplish that task. He would not even have to speak, "Let there not be a devil." Rather, all he would need to do is stop speaking, "Let there be a devil."

Jesus and the Devil

The devil is in the Father's hands. He always has been and always will be. But he is also under the absolute control of the Son. Consider first the temptation the devil presented Jesus in the wilderness. We are accustomed to seeing this confrontation as some sort of Old West shoot-out, complete with rolling tumbleweeds. The white-hatted Jesus rides into the corrupt town known as the earth, and the devil lays an ambush for him, right at his weakest moment. It's good versus evil, with the outcome in the balance. Such a scenario might make a grand movie, but it's not exactly how Scripture presents it.

First remember that this confrontation happened right after John the Baptist baptised Jesus, and the Father announced from heaven, "This is My beloved Son, in whom I am well pleased" (3:17). Jesus had been anointed as the Messiah. Like Adam at creation, Jesus had received the divine benediction; he had been declared good by the Father.

Chapter four of Matthew's Gospel begins: "Then Jesus was led up by the Spirit into the wilderness to be tempted by the devil" (v. 1). There was no ambush. It was the Spirit who directed Jesus to go into the wilderness. And more important, the Spirit did so with the purpose that this temptation would take place. It was planned from the beginning.

Whether the outcome could ever have been in doubt has been the occasion for debate among Reformed scholars. The great Charles Hodge argued that it could have gone either way: "The sinlessness of our Lord, however, does not amount to absolute impeccability. . . . If He was a true man He must have been capable of sinning. . . . Temptation implies the possibility of sin. If from the constitution of His person it was impossible for Christ to sin, then His temptation was unreal and without effect, and He cannot sympathize with His people" (Charles Hodge, *Systematic Theology*, vol. 2 [Grand Rapids: Eerdmans, 1946], 457).

Jonathan Edwards, on the other hand, provided two arguments, one directly, the other indirectly, that Jesus could not have sinned. Both are found in his essay "The

Freedom of the Will." First, Edwards argued that Jesus could not have sinned, because of the promises Scripture makes concerning him: "God had promised so effectually to preserve and uphold Him by His Spirit, under all temptations, that He should not fail of reaching the end for which He came into the world" (Jonathan Edwards, "The Freedom of the Will," part 3, section 2, in *The Works of Jonathan Edwards* [Carlisle, Pa.: Banner of Truth Trust, 1990], 42). Edwards then reminded his readers of several of those promises, including Matthew 1:21: "And she shall bring forth a Son, and you shall call His name Jesus, for He will save His people from their sins." Jesus could not have sinned in the wilderness, because such a sin not only would disqualify him as the redeemer of his people but also would require that he himself would need a redeemer.

The second argument is found in the overall thrust of "Freedom of the Will." In chapter 3 we talked about Edwards' argument that we always act according to our nature. We cannot do anything but that which is our strongest inclination at any given moment. Jesus, being wholly perfect, could not have had any sinful desires. Even a hint of a desire to disobey God is in itself a sin. That is not to say, however, that Jesus did not have desires with which to struggle in the wilderness. Let's look carefully at what happened.

> Then Jesus was led up by the Spirit into the wilderness to be tempted by the devil. And when He had fasted forty days and forty nights, afterward He was hungry. Now when the tempter came to Him, he said, "If you are the Son of God, command that these stones become bread." But He answered and

said, "It is written, 'Man shall not live by bread alone, but by every word that proceeds from the mouth of God.'" Then the devil took Him up into the holy city, set Him on the pinnacle of the temple, and said to him, "If You are the Son of God, throw Yourself down. For it is written, 'He shall give His angels charge concerning you,' and, 'In their hands they shall bear you up, lest You dash your foot against a stone.'" Jesus said to him, "It is written again, 'You shall not tempt the LORD your God.'" Again, the devil took Him up on an exceedingly high mountain, and showed Him all the kingdoms of the world and their glory. And he said to Him, "All these things I will give You if You will fall down and worship me." Then Jesus said to him, "Away with you, Satan! For it is written, 'You shall worship the LORD your God, and Him only shall you serve.'"

Matthew 4:1–10

Jesus had some perfectly righteous desires. The devil tempted Jesus to make bread from the stones. Surely after forty days and nights of fasting, Jesus had a desire for food. There would be nothing sinful in such a desire. Jesus did not, however, have to weigh his options. He knew the Father wanted him not to eat. Given the choice between eating and displeasing his Father, or waiting and pleasing his Father, there was no issue. Jesus didn't weigh, indeed couldn't have weighed, these competing options. His meat and his drink, as so wonderfully illustrated here, was to do the will of his Father.

No doubt Jesus also had a legitimite desire to prove to the devil that he was in fact the Son of God. Throwing himself off the pinnacle of the temple would have served that purpose. But it also would have been tempting the Father, something we are commanded not to do. Again Jesus, while having a legitimate desire, did not have any internal wrestling. He had no desire to displease the Father.

Finally the devil pulled out all the stops. He offered Jesus all the kingdoms of the world. We should remember that Jesus, in refusing this temptation, again did so while recognizing that those kingdoms were an utterly legitimate desire. The trouble was not with the kingdoms but the conditions. Those kingdoms were a motivation to Jesus. They were given to him at his ascension. The temptation was to receive the kingdoms in a way outside the covenant of redemption, the plan among the members of the Trinity from before time. The kingdoms would be his, not by bowing to the devil but by submitting to the will of the Father.

The word *temptation* has at least two meanings. It can be understood in both an active and a passive sense. It is possible, and indeed it happened here in the wilderness, for a person to be tempted and not tempted at the same time. The key is the different relationship. We can say, "Satan tempted Jesus," and, "Jesus was not tempted by Satan." A more personal example might help clear this up. How would you like to put this book down, get out your checkbook, and write me a check for everything you have? Does that sound tempting? I have offered you a temptation, yet you are not (at least I think you're not) tempted. In like manner the devil presented Jesus with a temptation, but Jesus was not tempted to take it.

Such a notion is hard for us to swallow. It is important not to denigrate the reality of the humanity of Jesus. His humanity has great import not only in terms of our salvation but also for our assurance. It is for this reason that the writer of Hebrews writes, "Seeing then that we have a great High Priest who has passed through the heavens, Jesus the Son of God, let us hold fast our confession. For we do not have a High Priest who cannot sympathize with our weaknesses, but was in all points tempted as we are, yet without sin" (Heb. 4:14–15). The Word itself reminds us of the great comfort we have in the temptation of Jesus. He was tempted in every way we are, we are told. But we mustn't leave off the last phrase, "yet without sin." Jesus was, as the Chalcedonian Creed reminds us, fully man. The trouble is that he was a very unusual man. We accept the old maxim "To err is human," though it is not strictly true. Since the fall, sin has been a constant presence in the lives of humans. But humanity doesn't exactly equal sin. Fallen humanity does. There are in heaven thousands upon thousands of people who do not sin. All we who have Christ in us long for the day when sin will be behind us.

Jesus, however, never had to wait. He had no inclination to sin, which is itself a sin. As such there was no foothold for the devil to work from. Yes, Jesus knows what it is like to be hungry, thirsty, tired, even fearful. What he has never experienced is sin. What he has never wondered is whether the devil is mightier than he.

Neither did the devils ever wonder. Mark's brief account of an exorcism gives us the clearest picture of Jesus' power over the forces of darkness. "Now there was a man in their synagogue with an unclean spirit. And he cried out, saying, 'Let us alone! What have we to do with You, Jesus of Nazareth? Did You come to destroy us? I know who You are—the Holy One of God!' But Jesus rebuked him, saying, 'Be quiet, and come out of him!' And when the unclean spirit had convulsed him and cried out with a loud voice, he came out of him" (Mark 1:23–26). This is the posture of the demons and, by extension, of the devil himself when confronted with the Holy One of God.

We need not fear the devil and his minions, for he who is in us is stronger than all the forces arrayed against him in the world. He is the one to whom has been given all authority on heaven and on earth.

The devil, then, is not mightier than God. He is under God's constant, absolute control.

*He is most holy in all his counsels,
in all his works, and in
all his commands. . . .*

Westminster Confession of Faith,
chapter 2, section 2

9

WHO IS GREATER?

Not Almighty over Himself

God is mighty over creation, mighty over the fall, over sweeping history and tiny details, over tyrants and over the devil, even mighty over "nothing." His might has overmatched everything we have looked at so far. Is there anything left in the created order over which he is not mighty? No. Is there anything left in the universe which can in any way limit his power? Yes. To see how that can be we will look at one of the greatest conundrums in the history of speculative theology.

Though no literal wars have ever been fought over this issue, it has certainly caused its share of headaches. There is a host of difficult questions, stumpers with which I, both as an undergraduate and as a seminarian, delighted in tormenting my professors. While some people like to debate how many angels can dance on the head of a pin, I prefer this classic teaser: Can God make a rock so big that even he can't move it?

The dilemma should be obvious. Answer this stumper in the affirmative and we have suggested there is something God cannot do, namely, move such a rock. Answer in the negative and again we have affirmed there is something God cannot do, namely, make such a rock. Just about everyone bristles at both of these options and recognizes there cannot be a *tertium quid,* a third option. It's one of those problems that can all too easily give one a charley horse between the ears.

God's Holy Will

Though I am no longer a student in school, I do have occasion to teach. Recently I had the privilege of teaching a group of home-schooled high schoolers the arcane art of logic. And on our first day of class I raised the issue of God and the rock. The speculation began in earnest, some students shouting out an affirmative, others equally zealous in the negative, but nearly all of them couldn't hide the puzzled looks on their faces. One young lady, however, did her teacher proud by calmly and quietly answering, "God can do all his holy will."

I would like to say I recognized the answer immediately as part of the Westminster Catechism. Instead, I am ashamed to admit I knew the words from some music my children listen to. Judy Rogers has made a number of recordings for children that get a lot of play in the Sproul house. Some set lessons from the Proverbs to music, others lessons from *Pilgrim's Progress,* and still another from the Westminster Catechism. It turns out the wise young lady in my logic class had also listened to Rogers. Answering the question of the rock, Rogers sings, "Is there anyone who can ever do anything that he wants to do? Yes, God can; God can do all his holy will."

There is a critical distinction between saying God can do anything and saying he can do all his holy will. The first statement has a problem in that it affirms God can do a host of things against his nature. Can God make another God, create an independent, noncontingent, uncreated being with the power of being within itself? Can God stop being God? Can God lie, or can he die? Can God make a shape which at the same time and in the same relationship has four straight lines of equal length and four right angles, and also has no sides and no angles; that is, can God make a square circle? Or to paraphrase our Father Abraham, can the judge of all the universe judge wrongly? These are old questions. The great Anselm, in his zeal to affirm an omnipotence that includes the possibility even of sinning, wrote in *Proslogium,* "But how art Thou omnipotent, if thou art not capable of all things? or, if Thou canst not be corrupted and canst not lie . . . how art Thou capable of all things? Or else to be capable of these things is not power but impotence. For he who is capable of those things is capable of what is not for his good, and of what he ought not to do and the more capable of them he is, the more power have adversity and perversity against him; and the less has he himself against these" (quoted in S. N. Deane, *St. Anselm* [La Salle, Ill.: Open Court, 1958], 14).

To answer these questions we have to go back to defining terms. What precisely do we mean by that word *can?* In some ways *can* is as difficult to define as *nothing.* Is God able to make a square circle or a rock he can't move? Well, yes and no. We can say yes because there is nothing outside himself which restrains him from doing so. God never says, "Well, I'd like to do X, but Y is restraining me. Wonder what I should do to remove Y." God never speaks this way because he is absolutely sovereign over all created things. Nothing in creation can restrain God, if only because, as he could do with the devil, all he need do to remove that restraint is to stop saying, "Let there be Y." There is nothing about squares or circles or rocks, in themselves, that would keep God from doing what he wills with them.

But we must also say no, he cannot do those things. While there is no restraint in the creation, there is restraint in the Creator. The only thing stopping God from making a square circle is God. You would not be far from the truth if you answered the big rock question by avoiding it with, "Why would he want to?" This evasion gets to the heart of the matter, the interaction of God's will and his character.

God's Will and His Character

Jonathan Edwards, in his essay "The Freedom of the Will," whether he intended to or not, gave great insight not only into the human will but also into the will in general, including the will of God.

Remember that Edwards defined the will as the mind choosing. And he affirmed that minds always choose according to the strongest inclination at the moment. And those inclinations always flow from the nature or character of the mind choosing. Edwards explained that while moral agents always have the natural ability to choose anything, they only have the moral ability to choose according to the chooser's nature.

If Edwards is right, God is bound to choose according to his nature, to do all his holy will. He cannot lie because to do so would be to act against his nature. He is truth, and thus cannot lie. The Bible also tells us God is not the source of confusion. He is a reasonable God and thus cannot create a square circle, a shape that at the same time and in the same relationship has both no sides and four sides. It is his nature to be almighty, and thus he cannot make a rock so big he cannot move it.

When we say God is omnipotent or almighty, we are saying not that he can do anything we can say but that he can do anything he wishes. Richard Swinburne, in his book *The Coherence of Theism* (Oxford: Clarendon Press, 1977), makes the distinction between things sayable and things doable: "A logically impossible action is not an action. It is what is described by a form of words which purport to describe an action, but do not describe anything which is coherent to suppose could be done. It is no objection to A's omnipotence that he cannot make a square circle. This is because 'making a square circle' does not describe anything which is coherent to suppose could be done" (p. 149). Note that Swinburne chooses his words carefully. He is not saying we may call omnipotent someone who cannot do actions which we imagine to be very difficult. He is saying that being unable to do actions which are incoherent does not disqualify someone from being omnipotent. Traversing the universe in a split second would be amazing indeed, and God could surely do it;

unlike making a square circle, it is not an incoherent idea.

In affirming that God cannot lie and that he cannot contradict himself, we are walking a very narrow line. We must be careful not to say God cannot lie because there is a moral law above him to which the Almighty is beholden. By the same token when we say God cannot contradict himself (by making a square circle), we are not saying that the rules of logic, by which A cannot be A and non-A in the same time and in the same relationship (the law of noncontradiction), somehow are above God, that he is beholden to them.

At the same time, we do not worship a capricious God. We do not want to affirm that God is above the law, that he can break his own rules of morality and truth willy-nilly. If such were the case, we could know nothing about God. If he were not bound by the law of non-contradiction or by the necessity of telling the truth, we could not believe anything he says. Without the law of noncontradiction, whenever the Bible affirms, "Believe on the Lord Jesus Christ, and you will be saved . . ." (Acts 16:31), it could at the same time be affirming, "Believe on the Lord Jesus Christ and you will be damned." If God were capable of lying, we could not know that when we appear before his throne he won't tell us that we're going to hell for embracing Jesus and that all those who have not embraced him will enjoy eternal felicity. Among the things Scripture lists that God cannot do is lie. We are told in Hebrews 6 first that "He could swear by no one greater" (v. 13) and second that "it is impossible for God to lie" (v. 18).

We avoid error when we affirm not that God is bound by laws transcendent to him, nor that he transcends law, but that he, and he alone, is autonomous—

literally, a law unto himself. He is bound, but only by himself. He is trustworthy, but only because it is his nature to be trustworthy.

We still have a question left to answer. This goodness which defines God's character, is it a product of his will, or does his will flow from it? A more common way of asking the question is this: Is God good because he wills to be so, or is good good because God wills it to be so? Can God decide, or could he have decided before all time, that it is good to lie? And if he had so decided, what would our obligation be toward this God? While it is true that God has not so decided, this hypothetical question is not strictly academic. How we answer determines how we see God. Do we worship God because he is God, or do we worship him because he is good?

Of course, we do both. We praise God both for his being, what he is, and for his grace, what he does. The first we call adoration; the second, thanksgiving. To try to separate the will of God and the character of God, however, is to deny his simplicity. Remember that God is one, as Deuteronomy 6:4 tells us. When we take the time to examine his attributes one at a time, we do so remembering that we cannot properly divide him and pit one part of him against another. As such, his will and his nature are ultimately one and the same. They are of a piece and cannot be separated.

When we say that God is bound by his nature, that he hasn't the moral ability (though he does have the natural ability, the power to make choices) to act against his nature, we are not suggesting God is in heaven feeling frustrated because he is just aching to sin or lie or die but cannot. With God there is no frustration, and there is no longing to do what he loathes. These "limitations" on God, that he cannot do what he does not want to do and cannot want what is against his nature, are not real limitations. To call doing what you do not want to do freedom is to confuse it with slavery. God is absolutely free and absolutely mighty.

The Paradox of God's Might

These are difficult issues. But it is necessary to grapple with them so we can know that what we read in God's Word is true and trustworthy, indeed that we can trust all he has revealed, both in the Word and in nature. Struggling with these issues equips us to do better that for which we were made, to worship him. Understanding that he is not mightier than himself, that his will and character are one, that he is a law unto himself, all these ideas help us to stand in greater awe of and wonder at God most high. They protect us from imagining either a god subservient to some transcendent law or an arbitrary and capricious god. They stop us, or rather ought to stop us, from wagging our finger at God for failing to attain a moral standard of our creation or imagination.

Remember how God responds to our impertinent demands that he obey our understanding of morality. Remember the wisdom Job showed when he decided silence was better than castigating the Almighty. God was quick to remind his inquisitor that he is God and answers to no one, that he is the potter and we are the clay. And a proper understanding will likewise keep us from the paralyzing fear that God will change as we change, that his love for us is as unsteady as our love for him.

There is no rock out there which God has made but is unable to move. There is no square circle from his hand. And there are no lies from the lips of God, no sweat upon his holy brow. There is no danger that he will pass away. And there are no outside limitations upon the Almighty One.

God does what he does precisely because he is what he is. His being and doing cannot be divided. "I am that I am," he is called. And he cannot stop being, nor can he desire to stop being, who he is.

In an awe-inspiring paradox (but never a contradiction), God is so almighty that the only thing over which his might does not extend is his might. All of creation is under his absolute control, and all of the Creator is one, a simplicity of perfection which cannot ever be imperfect.

*The most wise, righteous,
and gracious God doth oftentimes
leave, for a season, his own children
to manifold temptations,
and the corruption of their own
hearts, to chastise them for their
former sins, or to discover unto them
the hidden strength of corruption
and deceitfulness of their hearts,
that they may be humbled; and,
to raise them to a more close
and constant dependence for their
support upon himself, and to make
them more watchful against all
future occasions of sin, and for
sundry other just and holy ends.*

Westminster Confession of Faith,
chapter 5, section 5

10

Who Hurts?

Almighty over Suffering

The Puritans were a hardy bunch. While we tend to misremember history, thinking of the Puritan movement as an unstoppable juggernaut, the reality is the Puritans spent most of their glorious existence in less than glorious circumstances. They suffered horrible persecution in England and great hardship in America. But we don't, or at least ought not, admire them because they were a successful movement but rather because of their commitment to the Word of God. Their commitment was marked by a principle too often neglected in the modern church. Though they were erudite, studious, and produced some of the greatest minds and teachers in the history of Christ's church, perhaps what most set apart their thinking was their doing. The Puritans practiced a deep commitment to "reducing to practice" all that God had revealed.

We are all too eager to get to the practice. We want our teaching to be practical. But we don't often take the time to ground the practice in the Word. Thus we are told time and again we ought to spend our time not in discussions of the implications of God's sovereignty but out caring for the poor, the sick, the burdened, the suffering. The trouble with such practical counsel is that it doesn't work; it isn't practical.

The Puritans were eminently practical. They understood that Scripture was neither unrelated to life nor a mere plaything for the pleasant diversion of theological disputation. Scripture is the Word of God, God's revelation of who he is, who we are, and how God and man relate. It is a book of theology, and that theology tells us how to live our lives and how to think about our lives. Thus the desire to "reduce to practice" all the Scripture teaches is itself a reducing to practice of what Scripture teaches. The poor, the broken, the bereaved, what they need more than anything is sound theology. What is practical for all of us in the midst of suffering is to understand clearly how God relates to our suffering. Without an understanding of God's sovereignty over our suffering, we cannot understand the meaning of our suffering. And no suffering is worse than suffering which seems to be pointless.

Suffering and God's Goodness

The Puritans' suffering, commitment to the sovereignty of God, and diligence in reducing to practice what the Scripture teaches, then, were not unrelated.

The Puritans understood what we so often miss in our suffering, that the route to comfort (and, of course, the route to truth) is not to separate the suffering from the sovereignty of God but to recognize just how tightly bound they are.

In our age we think in terms of public relations. We are afraid people might not care for God if the truth were known about his relationship to suffering. Better to shield God from accusations that he is not loving and kind by making him impotent in the face of suffering. Better to comfort the afflicted with the idea that God is in his heaven full of sympathy, wishing the suffering would just go away but unable to make it happen.

The Christian church has accepted the devil's bargain. We have been told we must choose between these two options. Either God is all good but not all powerful, or all powerful but not all good. If God is all good, he would want there to be no suffering. So if there is suffering, he must be unable to stop it. Or perhaps God has the power to stop suffering but, because he is not good, does not exercise that power. The church has, by and large, opted for a good God who cannot stop suffering.

This argument, however, is fallacious. It presents a false dilemma. There are other options, but the way is blocked to the true option by the assumption of an unspoken and false premise. The argument assumes that a good God necessarily wouldn't want his creation to suffer. This assumption certainly appeals to us. Wouldn't it be great if God's goodness required that we experience no suffering? Wouldn't it be great if we could raise our fists toward God because he has failed to give us our due?

But the goodness of God does not preclude him from allowing suffering or pain. If anything, the difficult question is not how God could allow us to suffer but how he could allow us, who rebel against his majestic authority every day, who repay our Maker with incessant revolt, ever to experience pleasure. There is no logical problem of pain for sinners, only a problem of pleasure. The puzzler is why God would allow pleasure in the lives of we who hate him and do not obey his commands.

There once was a time, in the Garden before the fall, when there was no suffering. Then sin entered the world. And suffering necessarily came with it. If there had been no sin, there would be no suffering. Suffering doesn't just come because God sends it after we sin, but sin will always lead to suffering, because to sin is to act against our best interests. We need to remember that the law is for our immediate benefit. It exists not only for some future reward but for our best even now.

We must be careful, however, not to make the mistake of Job's "friends." They argued well against those who would say God must be either bad or powerless. Job would not have experienced suffering if he had been without sin. But we mustn't conclude we can measure the sinfulness of a person by the degree of his or her suffering. Job's friends argued essentially this way: "Whoa, Job! It's been a rough few days. You must have done something really terrible to deserve this." Did Job deserve what he went through? Be careful how you answer. No, he didn't. Job deserved far worse. Job's plight fell well short of what was due him, eternal damnation. Job was a sinner in the sense that all but Jesus are sinners. And all sinners deserve eternal damnation.

Because Job was a sinner we can rest assured he was dealt no injustice by God. In the midst of his suffering, he was in the arms of grace (as we all are in our suffering on earth). But Job was not a worse sinner than his friends, who suffered less. Though God never brings suffering in greater proportion than what is just, it does not follow that all suffering on earth is proportional to sin. God is not guilty of any wrongdoing in the story of Job. But neither is Job a particularly heinous sinner. To the contrary, God himself holds Job up comparatively as a paragon of virtue.

So as we look at the problem of suffering, we must keep in mind not only that we never suffer more than we deserve but also that our suffering does not serve as a barometer of sin.

Suffering and God's Sovereignty

Now that we have established that we should think about God and our suffering together, and a few things we should not think, what should we conclude about God and suffering?

First, God's sovereignty extends to our suffering. And that is not to say God merely permits suffering. Suffering is something God is actively involved in. Though it appears to get us out of some thorny thickets, the concept of God's having a permissive will is problematic. What do we mean when we say God permits something to happen? Often we mean that God, in his heart of hearts, doesn't want a thing to happen but will allow it for some other overriding concern. Some say, for instance, God permits us to suffer to teach us important lessons for our sanctification. God wants us to be holy, and suffering is what it sometimes takes. You may have heard someone say, or may have said yourself, something like, "God had to beat me over the head with such and such suffering for me to learn this lesson." Whenever a sentence begins with "God had to," be very careful. As we saw in the last chapter there are ways this can be true. "God had to" may mean, "Given God's nature, he had to." Or it may mean, "Given that God promised this, he had to do that." There is, for example, no reason within God which would make the hearing of the gospel a necessary condition for saving faith. Nor is there anything outside God which forced his hand, making him spread the faith through hearing the Word. But God did say, "Faith comes by hearing, and hearing by the word of God" (Rom. 10:17), and so we must conclude, No hearing, no faith.

The idea of a permissive will suggests that any event is spontaneous, that God looked down the corridor of time, saw some event which surprised him, and said, "Okay, I guess I'll let that happen." It sees the flow of history as a great movie which God did not write, produce, or direct but for which he merely served as the censor, giving his divine permisssion for it to happen. God does not permit; he ordains. He plans and executes his plan.

When we say, "God had to put me through this to teach me that," we may be communicating, "God used this suffering to teach me that lesson." That's not the same thing. Is it possible for God to bring you or me to the completion of our sanctification instantly? He has proven it is possible at the deaths of each of his saints. When we die, we are glorified, and a big part of that glorification is the completion of our sanctification. We will sin no more. Thus we know that suffering, while God may use it to serve the purpose of our sanctification, is not strictly necessary for our sanctification.

God doesn't have to use suffering for our sanctification, but he does. That is one of the purposes of suffering. We know this from the Word: "For whom the LORD loves He corrects, just as a father the son in whom he delights" (Prov. 3:12). Though we often don't appreciate it at the time, this is one of the ways God shows his love for us. Sometimes God uses direct immediate means to correct us, and sometimes indirect means. I have often prayed for humility this way: "Lord, please teach me humility, but please don't do it by humiliating me." I found out today that he is answering half of that prayer in the negative, half in the positive. The magazine I edit is about to be mailed to tens of thousands of people with a misspelling on the cover. God did not merely permit me to suffer this humiliation, he planned it (as he planned my prayers for humility).

There are all kinds of lessons to be learned from our suffering. We need to be reminded of our dependence on him. Countless men and women have testified that God taught them that very lesson, that they are dependent upon him, merely by taking away all the things they had mistakenly depended on. It is a hard lesson, but a powerful one.

Others need to be reminded of their sin. Frequently God sends us suffering directly related to particular sins. If I have been profligate with the money God has entrusted to me, he may just allow me to suffer some time in a pigsty to learn to be more careful, and more grateful.

And sometimes God sends suffering to remind us he is God. God sent Isaiah to tell Cyrus that God alone is God: "I am the LORD, and there is no other; there is no God besides Me. I will gird you, though you have

not known Me, that they may know from the rising of
the sun to its setting that there is none besides Me. I
am the LORD, and there is no other; I form the light and
create darkness, I make peace and create calamity..."
(Isa. 45:5–7). Here is no bare permission. God announces that he is the one who sends calamity.

God, however, does not use suffering only to teach.
Oftentimes he sends suffering to give us an opportunity to minister one to another. How can I give food to
the hungry, drink to the thirsty, and clothing to the
naked unless God makes someone to become hungry,
thirsty, and naked? While we're busy shaking our heads,
wondering what God is doing in allowing this suffering, too infrequently do we see it as an opportunity to
minister in his name.

The Ultimate Purpose of Suffering

But there yet remains one supreme reason God has
for sending suffering into our lives. It is the same ultimate reason for all he does. Jesus was walking with his
disciples and had occasion to teach this very lesson:
"Now as Jesus passed by, He saw a man who was blind
from birth. And His disciples asked Him, saying, 'Rabbi,
who sinned, this man or his parents, that he was born
blind?'" (John 9:1–2). One has to wonder what the disciples learned from their study of Job. The assumption
was there must have been a terribly grievous sin to war-
rant the blindness. Rather than castigating his disciples for their blindness on this issue, "Jesus answered,
'Neither this man nor his parents sinned, but that the
works of God should be revealed in him. I must work
the works of Him who sent Me while it is day; the night

is coming when no one can work. As long as I am in the world, I am the light of the world'" (vv. 3–5). Jesus pointed out a third option. The man was blind not because either he or his parents sinned but rather that God might be glorified in the healing of the man. This man suffered his whole life in blindness so Jesus could punctuate with a compelling object lesson the truth that he is the Light of the World. And Jesus healed the man.

There is the comfort in our suffering. It is not just that this is one case wherein the suffering served the purpose of glorifying God. All suffering, including that which also teaches us humility or patience, serves to glorify God.

Senseless suffering, if it could exist, is the great horror. But all suffering serves the highest purpose there is, the very purpose that our existence serves, the glorification of God. When we are in the midst of suffering, we must remember that in this ultimate sense all is right with the world. Things are operating as they should. The great theater of the glory of God is up and running in our little passion plays.

But it gets even better. In the darkest moments of our suffering, it is difficult for us to celebrate God's glory (though that is precisely what we ought to do, rejoicing in all things). When we are hurting we tend to be rather consumed with ourselves and find it difficult to say with much sincerity, "I sure am glad this horrible experience is glorifying you, Lord. Just let me know anytime I can serve in this capacity for you." But that's not all there is. We have an additional reason to celebrate in our suffering. We have an absolute, ironclad, law of the Medes and Persians guarantee from Jesus himself that nothing bad will ever happen to us.

Jesus commissioned the apostle Paul to write these words: "And we know that all things work together for good to those who love God, to those who are called according to His purpose" (Rom. 8:28). For too many of us these words have lost their power. They have become cliches. But they have become cliches because they are used so often, and they are used so often because they are so true and so comforting. We aggravate our suffering when we do not take this promise to heart. Or worse, we don't believe Paul. We pout and tell God we will not believe our suffering is for our good unless or until he tells us exactly how it works for our good.

And that brings us back to the danger in affirming God is sovereign and controls all things for his reasons. It doesn't follow that he is required to tell us his reasons. We may not know exactly what lesson we should be learning from a bout of suffering. We may have no idea how our suffering could ever be seen as good. And we may never on this earth see how God is glorified. But our inability to understand all of reality is no reason not to believe what God has revealed about reality. He has told us he is glorified in all the suffering across the world. And he has promised that the suffering of those who belong to him will work for their good. Faith is believing God. We need to believe him when he sends suffering into our path, and then we must praise his name and thank him for working for our good.

He is almighty over our suffering, using it to meet the penultimate goal of the well-being of his children and the ultimate goal of his own glory.

All those whom God
hath predestinated unto life,
and those only, he is pleased,
in his appointed and accepted time,
effectually to call, by his Word
and Spirit, out of that state of sin
and death, in which they are by
nature, to grace and salvation,
by Jesus Christ; enlightening their
minds spiritually and savingly
to understand the things of God,
taking away their heart of stone,
and giving unto them a heart
of flesh; renewing their wills, and,
by his almighty power, determining
them to that which is good,
and effectually drawing them
to Jesus Christ: yet so, as they come
most freely, being made willing by
his grace.

Westminster Confession of Faith,
chapter 10, section 1

11

WHO SAVES?

Almighty over Redemption

As people debate issues surrounding the sovereignty of God, no issue will continue to command as much of our attention as that in which sovereignty and salvation cross paths. Let God control creation, history, suffering, let him even control the path of every electron in the universe, but when it comes to our salvation, we prefer to drive. We want to take the wheel at the intersection of providence and predestination. This desire is rather ironic. To wish that we could be in control rather than God is sheer folly. But how much more so to want control when the issue is our eternal destiny? I know myself well enough to know I can't be trusted to decide who should win a football game. (Even I would probably be bored after ten or twenty years of the Pittsburgh Steelers never losing.) I sure don't want to be in charge when the stakes are heaven or hell.

God is the only one who can be trusted with such issues. And thankfully, like a dutiful parent with a screaming child who wants to drive the car, our Father in heaven has not and will not ever relinquish control. His hands are upon the wheel, and evermore shall be.

History and Redemption

God's sovereignty touches on our salvation in a number of ways outside predestination. We are saved by faith, and that faith involves a response to real historical events. But those historical events did not just happen. God brought to pass all that was necessary for our sins' atonement.

Luke, the historian, having recorded the announcements made to Zacharias and Mary, set for us the historical context: "And it came to pass in those days that a decree went out from Caesar Augustus that all the world should be registered. This census first took place while Quirinius was governing Syria. So all went to be registered, everyone to his own city" (Luke 2:1–3). Imagine you were a pious Jew at this time. Your history includes the promise to Abraham, a famine which drove Jacob and his sons to Egypt, centuries of slavery there, followed by the glory of the exodus. Then came the conquest of the Promised Land, turmoil under the judges, the pinnacle of your glory in David and Solomon, then a pattern of apostasy and repentance that degenerated ultimately until the exile. Finally there was a glorious return to the land, but not long after, the Romans rolled into town.

You are bound to be frustrated, to wonder why God would allow the Romans to occupy the land he gave to you. Some of your recent ancestors, though the odds were so much against them and perhaps born of a pious faith in God's ability to deliver, fought and died in a vain attempt to drive out the Romans. You may yet have friends or relatives among those still plotting against Rome.

Rome, you understand, is unlike any power before it. This empire extends over the known world, with the exception of those barbaric Celts in the North Sea. Why would God allow such a tragedy?

Hopefully you wouldn't ask such a question. You would know first that God didn't merely allow it but brought it to pass. And though you couldn't see how, you would trust that God was working things out for your good and his glory. What you probably couldn't understand is that this very tragedy, the conquest of the world by the Roman army, and all that went with it, would be the means through which God would effect not only your redemption but the fulfillment of the promise to your father Abraham that he would be a blessing to all the nations of the world.

And if you did trust God regarding the Roman occupation, you might find yourself fretting over the agitators in your camp, those who plot rebellion and in the process provoke Rome to wrath. You might not trust God about those who don't trust God. While you might grieve over the sins of your brothers, you might not realize that even this would be necessary for the Good News to spread.

Consider all these "coincidences" of history. None but the Romans had practiced the barbarism of crucifixion. Yet we were told centuries before by Moses, "Anyone who is hung on a tree is under God's curse" (Deut. 21:23 NIV). The Roman empire was the first which could carry out a worldwide decree such as the one which sent Joseph back to the sleepy town of Bethlehem, where it had been prophesied the Messiah would be born. The Roman army travelled on its feet, creating the greatest road system the world had ever known. This and the "Pax Romana" (Roman peace) allowed for greater travel and communication, giving opportunity for the message of the gospel to reach the four corners of the known world.

Even the agitation against Rome served to spread the gospel. First, it caused the people to look for Messiah, one who would remove the burden of Roman rule. Second, it allowed for the people to become disappointed, such that they would turn on Jesus when he failed to meet their expectations. And the assault on Jerusalem in 70 A.D. by the Roman army scattered believers all over the world. With them went the Good News.

God ordered all these circumstances for the purpose of redeeming his people. But of course, his sovereignty doesn't stop there. If Edwards is right, that we always act according to our strongest inclination, and if we are fallen to such an extent that we have no desire to do anything good, then God will have to act to get his people to embrace all that he accomplished in the life, death, and resurrection of Jesus. How can men and women who are dead in their trespasses and sins, who do only evil, ever do the good thing of responding in faith to the gospel? God would have to intervene.

Faith and God's Intervention

And he does intervene. Scripture tells us the flesh profits nothing (John 6:63). There is nothing in us that will do us any good. We cannot even recognize our need for salvation, outside the work of God. Jesus warned his listeners, "Do not murmur among yourselves. No one can come to Me unless the Father who sent Me draws him; and I will raise him up at the last day" (John 6:43–44).

One of the challenges for the students in the logic class I teach is translating ordinary language into a form that is easier to use in logical categories, the better to test their validity. Jesus here makes it easy for them by presenting a "universal negative," a category of zero. In the category of those who can come to Jesus, there are none who come without first being drawn by the Father. Jesus does not here say that all who are drawn by the Father come. Some, wishing to avoid the trap of Pelagianism, the heresy that men are morally neutral and have it in them to save themselves, use this text to defend what is known as prevenient grace. Prevenient grace is grace which "comes before"; it comes to all men before any come to faith. People who affirm this idea posit that the Father gives grace to all men. They hold that Jesus is saying here that all men are drawn of the Father. Some respond in faith and others do not. There are several difficulties with this scenario, some philosophical, others exegetical. If the Father draws all in the same measure and some come while others do not, the difference between coming and not coming must lie with the individual. This, of course, isn't a problem for some. That is their goal, to leave the steering wheel in the hands of the individual. But we must ask, what accounts for the difference?

When I am engaged in disagreements with folks over the sovereignty of God in redemption, what some call predestination and others the doctrines of grace (and what Jimmy Swaggart calls a doctrine from the pit of hell), I often find myself playing dueling verses. I present the above passage, and others that we will look at, while my opponent presents passages in which men are called to repent and believe. (The predestinarian position never denies that men must choose.) To cut through the muddle, I often say something like this: "You and I together hear a presentation of the gospel. You repent and believe, while I do not. According to your position, God treats us the same. So why did you believe while I did not? Are you better than me? Are you smarter than me?" My opponent is in a dilemma. He or she recognizes that it is a good thing to embrace the gospel and a bad thing to reject it. But most folks, while wanting to maintain control, are wisely reluctant to boast. Ascribe the difference to man and there is boasting. Ascribe it to God and you have become a predestinarian. Ascribe it to chance and you have spoken nonsense and made eternity a matter of rolling the dice.

That reluctance to boast is not mere pious humility but is rooted in Scripture. Paul writes to the saints at Ephesus, "For by grace you have been saved, through faith, and that not of yourselves; it is the gift of God, not of works, lest anyone should boast" (Eph. 2:8–9).

Unless faith is the gift of God, those with faith have reason to boast.

Paul also highlights the impossibility of men coming to faith on their own in the same chapter. He writes, "And you He made alive, who were dead in trespasses and sins . . ." (Eph. 2:1). That is the condition of men apart from the sovereign work of God. We are dead, and dead men don't do anything, let alone muster the goodness to come to faith on their own. The "you" to whom Paul is speaking is specific. The letter is addressed, "To the saints who are in Ephesus, and faithful in Christ Jesus" (1:1). These are the ones who have been given faith. Paul very clearly differentiates between his audience and the world in verses 2 and 3 of chapter 2: "in which you once walked according to the course of this world, according to the prince of the power of the air, the spirit who now works in the sons of disobedience, among whom also we all once conducted ourselves in the lusts of our flesh, fulfilling the desires of the flesh and of the mind, and were by nature children of wrath, just as the others" (2:2–3). It would be difficult for Paul to make the contrast more clear. God hasn't made all alive. There are others.

Frequently what motivates this tendency to place the decisive factor in the hands of men is not an impetuous desire to get credit. Rather, many embrace an Arminian view (that God ultimately wills all men to be saved but that man's will trumps God's will) of this matter out of a sincere, understandable, but ultimately misguided attempt to shield God against the accusation of unfairness. Somehow we believe that God has an obligation to treat all people the same way. If he is going to change some people's nature, such that they embrace the gospel, it is incumbent upon him to do the same for all. There is a strong egalitarian streak in us, and we expect God to act accordingly. The trouble with this understandable view is that God goes to great lengths to make sure we don't think this about him.

God's Mercy

God deals with people differently. To be sure, God loves all mankind. He made us all, and we all bear his image. That love, however, does not preclude God from loving people in different ways. We are all called to love all men, our neighbors and our enemies. But husbands are also called to love their wives, and that not in the same way we love our neighbors. Can my neighbor or my enemy bring charges against me because I do not love him or her in the same way I love my wife and children?

Consider the exodus. Did God appear to Pharaoh in the same way he appeared to Moses? Did he treat the two the same? God blessed Moses. He made covenant with Moses. He cursed Pharaoh, hardening his heart and making war against him. But some might argue God treated these men differently because they were different men, Moses good and Pharaoh wicked.

Such a perspective would certainly get God off the hook of being unfair. But it would not do the same with respect to Jacob and Esau. Paul makes this very point: "And not only this, but when Rebecca also had conceived by one man, even by our father Isaac (for the children not yet being born, nor having done any good or evil, that the purpose of God according to election might stand, not of works but of Him who calls), it was said to her, 'The older shall serve the younger.' As it is

written, 'Jacob I have loved, but Esau I have hated'"
(Rom. 9:10–13). Paul here eliminates two means of
escaping the charge that God treats people differently.
He explicitly denies that God made his choice based
on anything Jacob or Esau had done. It would be dis-
honest to sneak the works of Jacob and Esau in here by
suggesting that while they had not yet done anything,
God foreknew what they would do. The reason for
God's choice is given here. It is not because of his foreknowledge that it would stand. It is because it was his
purpose.

God's electing love distinguishes among people, but
not because of any merit in those chosen. What should
we say then? Is there unrighteousness in God? Funny
you should ask. Paul raises that very question. Here is
his answer: "Certainly not! For He says to Moses, 'I will
have mercy on whomever I will have mercy, and I will
have compassion on whomever I will have compassion.' So then it is not of him who wills, nor of him who
runs, but of God who shows mercy" (Rom. 9:14–17).

Mercy, by definition, cannot be obligated. Imagine,
if you will, that you and ten of your friends bought this
book on the same day in the same bookstore. Each of
your friends announces his or her delight in opening
the book to find a fresh hundred-dollar bill. You, of
course, grab your book and carefully turn each page.
Alas, there is no bill in your copy. Have I or the bookstore or the publisher done you any wrong? Do you have
any standing to lodge a complaint? What if ten thou-
sand people found such a bill and you did not? You say
to the bookstore manager, "My bill was missing. Could
something have happened to it?" And the manager
says, "Oh, there was no bill for you." You might suggest,
"Are these others better than me, smarter?" And he or

she might say, "Not at all. I have my reasons for how I chose, but they have nothing to do with anyone's merit." Should (not would, but should) you complain?

How much more so with God. Sovereignty goes beyond mere power. The concept is not just that God is strong enough to do anything he wishes but that he has the right, the authority, to do so. There are no oughts with God beyond his holy will. And, as shown by Moses and Pharaoh, and as Paul tells us, God almighty reserves his right to show mercy to whom he will.

God manifests his sovereign power in our salvation first by bringing to pass the historical events that make it possible. His rule over creation, over the fall, over the great sweep of history and the tiniest details, even his sovereign control over the suffering in this world (most particularly the suffering of his Son) all work together for the winning of his elect. But before he executed his plan, he planned to choose some while passing by others. He chose those to whom he would show mercy.

But he doesn't stop there. The Bible doesn't teach justification by election. By no means. Though none come who were not first chosen, we come in faith. We enter God's grace by trusting the finished work of Christ alone. And here he works as well. God the Father chooses. God the Son dies for his bride. And God the Holy Spirit sovereignly and efficaciously enters the hearts of the elect and changes them. He quickens those whom he will, giving life to the dead. The work of regeneration is the Spirit changing our wicked inclinations such that we then freely embrace the gospel. It is indeed our faith. He does not have faith for us. But it is a faith which he first gave to us, even when we didn't want it.

Remember that while we were dead, we could do nothing good. (In fact, we could do nothing at all.) Our inclinations were only evil. If the Spirit had showed up at our door and asked, "Would you like to trust in the work of Jesus, to embrace him as Lord and Savior?" we would have slammed the door on his face. And so we did, until he changed us. And so do those who hear the Good News and do not believe.

First he must change us, on his own, without asking or being asked. Then we freely, in accordance with our new nature, embrace the gospel. He is almighty over our redemption, and he is still at work, fulfilling his promise to Abraham, sovereignly changing the "all who are afar off." If he had not, we would be without hope and destined for an eternity of God's righteous judgment.

He promised in the Garden that the seed of the woman would crush the head of the serpent. And he has brought it to pass by his might. And then he began a new work of creation that continues each time the Spirit breathes life into we who once were his enemies. Here is where his power is most important, and most tender. Here is where we have the greatest reason to praise his great might. We would do well not to seek any of the glory for ourselves.

*In which war, although
the remaining corruption,
for a time, may much prevail; yet,
through the continual supply
of strength from the sanctifying
Spirit of Christ, the regenerate part
doth overcome; and so, the saints
grow in grace, perfecting holiness
in the fear of God.*

Westminster Confession of Faith,
chapter 13, section 3

12

Who's Batting Cleanup?

Almighty in Sanctification

The ultimate and penultimate reasons for all God does join in our sanctification. Remember God does all things ultimately for his glory. And he does all things penultimately for the well-being of his church. Just as he was not finished with his creation once he created it, so he is not finished with us when he re-creates us. The regenerating work of the Spirit is only the beginning.

Justification and Sanctification

There is a great dispute between Roman Catholics and Protestants about the relationship of justification and sanctification. The Protestant faith affirms that first the Spirit works a new heart in us such that we embrace the atoning work of Christ. That faith appropriates the work of Christ such that our sin is covered by his death. The penalty due us for our sins was paid by Christ at Calvary. In like manner the obedience of Christ is deemed ours. At that point, we stand before God forensically justified. God declares us just, though in ourselves we are not yet just. (Rome calls this a legal fiction.)

From there we grow in grace. We become in ourselves more and more what God has declared us to be. We begin our sanctification, or our "holification." That process reaches its end at our death. At that point we are glorified, a change that focuses principally on the completion of our sanctification—that is, we are holy in ourselves.

Heaven is full of great wonders and joys. One which excites me is this glorification. Imagine never sinning again. Imagine no more struggles. Imagine pleasing God in all you do. That is where we are headed, even now.

In the Roman view we must work our way to justification. God cannot, according to Rome, declare us just until we are just in ourselves. But Rome rejects Pelagianism. God infuses grace into us just to make sure. This grace from God is a powerful aid in the person as he or she works toward perfection. If the Roman Catholic is not yet perfect at death, the sins which remain must be purged in purgatory. When that is complete, the Catholic can go to heaven.

Some suggest that the Reformation was merely a semantic problem, that what the Reformers meant by justification and sanctification is the same as what

Rome meant by justification. While such confusion is understandable, it is nevertheless off base. The Reformed view is that we are justified by an alien righteousness, a righteousness not our own, while Rome claims that the righteousness must be our own.

The issue becomes even more complicated when we consider how that righteousness is appropriated. The Reformation slogan *sola fide,* faith alone, was no mere slogan but was one of the two driving factors in the Reformation. (The other is *sola scriptura,* Scripture alone, the idea that Scripture alone can bind the conscience of the believer.) Protestants affirm we are justified by faith alone and not by works. The Counter-Reformation meeting, the Council of Trent, argued that such a view encouraged a disregard of the law, that Christians would not be motivated to obedience. Martin Luther disagreed. He argued that while we are justified by faith alone, it is never by a faith that is alone. Works must follow. No works, no faith.

According to Luther these works are in no way the ground of our salvation, but they are necessarily present. We all know that where there is smoke, there is fire. But smoke is not what does the burning, fire is. We must be careful with the analogy, however. We do not say that where there are works, there is faith. Works are not a sufficient condition for faith but a necessary result.

If the Spirit is not working in us, we can be sure we are not in the faith. This is the point of James, who warns, "But do you want to know, O foolish man, that faith without works is dead?" (James 2:20). But where do these good works come from?

We affirmed that in the work of regeneration, the Spirit acts alone. He changes our hearts without our asking or giving permission or our cooperation in any way. It is a monergistic work, a work of one. The same is not true of our sanctification. It is a work of synergism, a cooperative effort between man and God. Paul encourages the Philippians, "Therefore, my beloved, as you have always obeyed, not as in my presence only, but now much more in my absence, work out your own salvation with fear and trembling" (Phil. 2:12). If we were to stop here, we might get the idea that our sanctification is a monergistic work, of man and not God. Paul exhorts believers to work. But he doesn't stop there, "for it is God who works in you both to will and to do for His good pleasure" (v. 13). We are to work hard in our sanctification because God is working in us.

That we are working together is important for a number of reasons. First, it again gives us reason to praise God. He is to be glorified because of the work he does in us. Second, it reminds us where we need to turn in the face of our failures. I try to remind my children of this when I discipline them. When my children disobey, they are punished. After they secure my forgiveness, we pray together. We always cover the same three concepts in our prayers. First is repentance for the sin. Last is an expression of gratitude for the work of Christ in covering our sins. But in between we ask that God's Spirit be at work in us such that we will be better empowered to obey. Of course, this is not just for children. We all ought to go through these steps as we confess our sins.

But perhaps the third reason is the most important: it gives us assurance of our salvation.

Assurance

Remember in chapter 1 we talked about God's immutability. He never changes. Such a notion just highlights all the more how much we change. Our faith is what appropriates the work of Christ. That faith is a gift sovereignly given by God. But it is our faith after that. And knowing the power of sin that yet remains in us, it is only natural that we would fear we might mishandle this faith, even lose it.

I lose things. My work associates know that if they want me to have something, it is wisest for them to keep it for me. My assistant keeps copies of every paper she gives me, because she knows me. I try to treat some things given to me more carefully than others. But even so, I might worry that this faith God gave me, the very faith that assures me of eternal life, might be something I would lose. It is because the Spirit is working with us in all his sovereignty that I can rest assured in my salvation.

Paul combines the doxological element of this synergy with its power in terms of assurance in this same letter: "I thank God upon every remembrance of you, always in every prayer of mine making request for you with all joy, for your fellowship in the gospel from the first day until now, being confident of this very thing, that He who has begun a good work in you will complete it until the day of Jesus Christ . . ." (Phil. 1:3–6).

That is the same confidence we need, and we need to remember it is rooted in him. The word *assurance,* like the word *tempt,* has nuances. Assurance can refer either to that which makes a thing sure or that which makes us know it is sure. It's the same with *justifica-*

tion. If I asked you to justify your justification, you would see the distinction. It is faith in Christ which appropriates Christ's justice for you, your fruit which justifies your belief that you have faith. This is James' point in his epistle.

In what do you trust for your salvation? It is Christ who makes it sure. He is our surety. He is the objective part of our assurance. The subjective part is our experience of that sureness.

But Jesus is our surety not only in the sense that he has truly earned our salvation. Not only has he paid for us, but he has the strength to keep us. It is because he is almighty that we can never lose what he has given. This not only follows from the promise made through Paul that all things work for good to those who love him (what could be worse than to lose one's salvation?), but Jesus himself makes an even more specific promise: "My sheep hear My voice, and I know them, and they follow Me" (John 10:27). Jesus affirms that those who are his will grow in grace. We follow him, and not the ways of the world. But it gets even better: "And I give them eternal life, and they shall never perish; neither shall anyone snatch them out of My hand. My Father, who has given them to Me, is greater than all; and no one is able to snatch them out of My Father's hand" (vv. 28–29).

Here in essence we have a promise bound by a strength that is three times almighty. The Spirit is at work in us, such that we who are his follow him. Nothing and no one is stronger than the Spirit. Jesus grants us eternal life, and nothing and no one can take us from his hand. And we are given by the Father, and nothing and no one can take us from him.

Again Jesus makes our reasoning easier. He gives us a universal negative. What is in the category of things which can take us from him? Nothing, and here nothing is the reality, not the concept. One need not fear that nothing or no one will someday sneak up on Jesus and snatch us from him.

Of course, some seek a way out of this text, to leave open the possibility of wiggling out of Jesus' hand. Some who deny that the true Christian will always stay a Christian suggest that the text implies one can escape on one's own. After all, one doesn't "snatch" oneself. This is desperation. Who would want out of Christ's hands more, one who is in them or the devil? If the devil cannot get us out, we will not get ourselves out. Jesus gives a universal negative and does not exclude the individual.

But what about our experience? How can we rest in his strength, be assured he will keep us to the end, when we see so many leaving the faith?

I must confess to having my own assurance challenged when those whom I once saw as heroes in the faith turned their back on the faith. Two men who discipled me in Christ, who communicated with wisdom and zeal the biblical truths of the Reformed faith, who watched out for my very soul, have since rejected that same faith. These two did not slip quietly into skepticism but have noisily embraced another faith that calls the gospel of justification by faith alone a damnable heresy. If these men whom I looked up to can turn, how can I have any assurance for myself? What is to keep me from turning?

True Believers

The same John who recorded this potent promise from Jesus knew something of the same experience.

We tend to see the first century of the church as an idyllic time of peace and orthodoxy. But it was not so. And like me, many who remained in the church wondered about those who had wandered away. John explained, "They went out from us, but they were not of us; for if they had been of us, they would have continued with us; but they went out that they might be made manifest, that none of them were of us" (1 John 2:19). John belabors what is a fairly simple point. If they left, they were never here. In fact, John gives a pretty clear syllogism, if P then not Q. P therefore not Q. If they left, they were not believers. They left, therefore they were not believers.

It yet troubles us because of the limitations of assurance regarding other people. In the church I pastor, those who desire to join must come before the elders and make what is known as a credible profession of faith. They are not required to prove they are believers. They could not do so, as we do not see the hearts of others. If they say that they believe the gospel, that they trust in the finished work of Christ, and if we know of no heinous, unrepentant sins (that is, they appear to follow the voice of the Shepherd), then a judgment of charity says we are to treat them as believers. If they later deny that Jesus died for their sins or are unrepentant in the face of church discipline, we do not conclude, "Here is a Christian who lost his or her salvation, who wiggled out of Christ's mighty hand." Rather we affirm, because of John, that these were never believers. A credible profession of faith is not the same as the actual possession of faith. One's profession can be proven to be no longer credible, but actual possession is never lost.

There are degrees of assurance. We can worry that we lack saving faith. We ought to worry when we are in sin. When David gave orders for the death of Uriah, when Peter slunk away after his third denial, they must have, or at least should have, asked, "How can I be a child of God and do such things?" As our fruit grows more and more moldy, we ought to begin to doubt our salvation. But we ought never to doubt that those who believe will be saved. Just as there are different degrees of assurance, so there are different degrees of doubt. Luther, after crawling up the cathedral stairs on his knees, is said to have muttered, "Who knows if it is true?" Asking if the gospel is true is a very different thing than asking if I truly have faith. And to affirm that it is true, and that you do have faith, but yet to worry that you could lose what you have, that too is a problem.

The answer to all of these concerns is to remember how strong he is. He is strong enough to communicate clearly through his Word and to authenticate that message with great works of might—miracles. He is strong enough to invade our wills and change us on his own. He is strong enough to hold on to us, despite the efforts of the devil and any efforts we might make to escape. And he is strong enough to work in and through us to do his will such that we bear the fruit for which he made us.

Paul connects these works of God's might: "For whom He foreknew, He also predestined to be conformed to the image of his Son, that He might be the firstborn among many brethren. Moreover whom He predestined, these He also called; whom He called, these He also justified; and whom He justified, these He also glorified" (Rom. 8:29–30). Note what happens when we try to separate these works. What if he predestined only some of those he foreknew? (By the way, it would probably be more accurate to refer to this first group as those he fore-loved. If the "knowing" here means a mere having of information and not the knowing of love, as when husbands are said to "know" their wives and they conceive, then all men would be glorified, and hell would be empty.) Then some objects of his love would not have been predestined. He would have failed. And if only some that he predestined are called, again he would have failed. And if only some that he called were justified, he would have failed. And if only some he justified would be glorified, he failed.

There is our assurance. We enter the middle, because we cannot know God's secret will in advance. If we have faith, we know we have been loved, predestined, and called first. Having the faith, we are now justified and look forward with eager anticipation to our glorification. We can get down in our sin. We can get frustrated with the slow progress we are making in our sanctification. But we ought to trust in his almighty strength. He will not let us go, and no one is strong enough to take us from him. And he predestined us not only to be in heaven but to be conformed to the image of his Son, the firstborn of the new creation. He does not fail, for he is almighty. That is why we know that "He who has begun a good work in you will complete it until the day of Jesus Christ . . ." (Phil. 1:6).

*The doctrine of this high mystery
of predestination is to be handled
with special prudence and care,
that men, attending the will of God
revealed in his Word, and yielding
obedience thereunto, may, from
the certainty of their effectual
vocation, be assured of their eternal
election. So shall this doctrine afford
matter of praise, reverence,
and admiration of God;
and of humility, diligence,
and abundant consolation to all
that sincerely obey the gospel.*

Westminster Confession of Faith,
chapter 3, section 8

WHO'S IT GONNA BE?

Almighty over Eternity

We began our look at how strong God is by raising some warnings. Some folks engage in theological exploration for the sake of mere intellectual amusement or to prove their own wisdom. Others, confusing immature faith with childlike faith, shrink from the meatier questions of theology. Have we fallen off either side of the horse? Do we look at what we have covered in this book and say either, "Wow, that was fun. Let's do quantum physics next time?" or, "So what? Such discussions lead only to division and have no practical value. Give me news I can use."

To assess whether we have made good use of our time, we must ask, Is what we discussed in this book true? Though no one seems to be able to locate the source of this bit of wisdom, apparently John Calvin once said that at our best we are correct 80 percent of the time in our theology. And remember, that's Calvin. I'm no Calvin. So why don't I go back and excise all those ideas in this book that are wrong, whether it be 25 percent or 75? The problem is that we never know which parts of the things we believe are the erroneous ones. While we always believe we are right in what we affirm, we do not believe we are always right in what we affirm. Each proposition we affirm, we affirm because we believe it to be true. If you could lay out every belief of mine on a table, point at each, one by one, and ask me, "Do you believe this to be true? How about this one? And the next?" at each point I would say yes. And if you were then to sweep your arm across the total of my beliefs and ask me, "Is all this correct?" I would have to answer, "Of course not."

This dilemma ought not force us to stop making assertions, to push us into a relativism or skepticism that suggests, "No one really knows anything for sure anyway, so never mind." We do know several things with certainty. We know that God's Word is utterly reliable, that all it says, each affirmation as well as the whole, is true. And we know that the Bible does not fail to communicate what it says. And we must conclude two more truths from these true propositions. The first is that we have a duty to understand all we are able in his Word. The Bible is a great gift from God, revealing who he is. The second is that we have a duty to test our understanding of the Word with the Word.

The Reformers taught as their fundamental rule of biblical interpretation the "analogy of faith," that Scripture interprets Scripture. We do not judge the truthfulness of what we affirm about God's strong right arm by what our denomination affirms, by what our pastor affirms, or by what we would like to believe, what makes us comfortable. The Bible is the judge. All of our propositions must appear in this court. No other has jurisdiction.

That obligation falls on both of us. It is my duty to test all I write against Scripture. You, however, are not exempt from doing the same. You are called to be as noble as the Bereans, checking all things against the Word. You are not to shrug and say, "Well, I'll ask God how strong he is when I get to heaven, and therefore I need not ask now." You will ask. And there in heaven, though we will not be omniscient, we will be glorified. God's work in our sanctification will be complete, and so there will not be even 20 percent error in our thinking.

But thinking on God's great strength will not be all we will be doing. We will be reveling in it. We will be awed by it. We will be praising God for it. That is our destiny, if in fact we are in his strong right arm. We will be consumed with the glory of his holiness, his oneness, his almightiness. That is what we are for.

The Story of History

Remember where we began. There once was God and nothing else. Desiring to manifest his great power and glory, God determined to create the world and the people in it, some on whom he would exercise his great wrath and justice, some on whom he would exercise his great power and grace. The final scene of this great theater is the separation of these two elements of the play. Those in the first group will be cast into the outer darkness, a place where they will experience the full avenging justice of the Father forever. Those in the second group, however, will live forever in the presence of the almighty Playwright. There we will sing his praises, recognize his glory (though never fully, for the finite cannot contain or grasp the infinite), and wonder at his strength forevermore.

To get from that beginning to that ending, from that alpha to that omega, the Almighty spoke by the power of his word and brought into being that which was not. While the scope of the universe is cause for great wonder, perhaps we ought to be more moved by sheer amazement that anything was made at all. He filled his creation out of the fullness of his glory. And on the sixth day, he made man. He placed him in a garden and made covenant with him, laying down his law.

And then, so he might show wrath and mercy, he brought to pass the fall of man. When he returned to his garden, however, he revealed, however vaguely, the great plan of redemption, that the seed of the woman, in having his heel bruised, would crush the head of the serpent.

From there he worked out this plan, weaving together events both great and small. By his great might he sent a famine in the land and sent Joseph to the court of Pharaoh. He brought his chosen people into Egypt and put them under the heel of Pharaoh. Why? To show his power in setting them free. He worked great miracles, until the end when he sent death throughout the land, but not before giving more information on the seed of the woman, he who would be the Lamb without blemish.

He led his people through the wilderness and vanquished those who yet lived in the land of promise. He again sent a famine, sending Elimelech to Moab, where his sons married. Naomi returned with Ruth, and through the ministrations of the law and God's providence came marriage to Boaz, then the birth of Obed, who begat Jesse, who begat David. David ascended the throne and prepared the way for the true King.

Apostasy came, and the great powers among the Gentiles humbled God's people by taking them in exile and then were themselves humbled by God's great strength. Meanwhile, a people grew in the peninsula across the sea. God raised up Rome to conquer the world and prepare it for the invasion of the incarnation and the spread of the Good News. This same God ordained that his Son should be crucified. It pleased him to bruise the Son.

But death be not proud. For not even death is stronger than our God, and the tomb could not hold him. Our mighty God broke the bonds of death, and in so doing broke the bonds of sin and crushed the head of the serpent, just as he had promised.

Forty days passed, and Jesus ascended his throne and sent the other Comforter, even his Spirit. The Spirit gave power to the message and took it to every corner of the world. Even now he works, giving life to the dead, shining light in the darkness, bringing forth fruit in the barren.

The Story Goes On

Is the story over, then? Have we reached its end? By no means. The great drama of the glory of God goes on. And this is our part: "Go therefore and make disciples of all the nations, baptizing them in the name of the Father and of the Son and of the Holy Spirit, teaching them to observe all things that I have commanded you; and lo, I am with you always, even to the end of the age" (Matt. 28:19–20).

We can do this with great confidence. The same Jesus who gave this charge is more than mighty enough to bring it to pass. He not only has the power but the authority. He prefaced his charge to the disciples with this critical truth of his ascension: "All authority has been given to Me in heaven and on earth" (Matt. 28:18). As we look through the mighty works of God recorded for us in his mighty book, we are to learn from them not what he once was capable of doing but what he continues to do even now.

We are in the midst of great suffering. Christ's church is weak, downtrodden, and oppressed. Around the world Christians are being destroyed for their faith. But this is not the first time, nor is it any evidence of weakness in our God. It has been thus from the beginning of Christ's church. Nero once lit his garden parties with the burning bodies of the faithful. The coliseums were filled with sports fans who gathered to watch our brothers and sisters destroyed by wild beasts.

When Rome fell, those who survived turned their rage at the Christians and their strange God, blaming them for the calamity. The Waldenses, the precursors of the Protestants, were killed by the tens of thousands by the Pope and his minions. Hus was burned for the crime of preaching the gospel. Then came the Reformation, and with it the scourge of war.

In Scotland the monarchy hunted down the Reformers. They practiced the cruelest barbarisms, tying women to stakes set in the sea and watching them drown as the tide came in. Today in America Christians are carted off to jail for the crime of home-schooling their children to better instruct them in the faith. In Central and South America missionaries are in danger both from Marxist guerrillas and Roman Catholic authorities, while in some Muslim countries Christians are killed as an expression of faith in Allah.

But our God never changes. He never grows weak or weary. It was to persecuted Christians that God spoke through his servant John. He gave no image of a God wringing his hands, desperately trying to find a way to stop the persecution. Rather John wrote,

> Then I saw heaven opened, and behold, a white horse. And He who sat on him was called Faithful and True, and in righteousness He judges and makes war. His eyes were like a flame of fire, and on His head were many crowns. He had a name written that no one knew except Himself. He was clothed with a robe dipped in blood, and His name is called The Word of God. And the armies in heaven, clothed in fine linen, white and clean, followed Him on white horses. Now out of His mouth goes a sharp sword, that with it He should strike the nations. And He Himself will rule them with a rod of iron. He Himself treads the winepress of the fierceness and wrath of Almighty God. And He has on His robe and on His thigh a name written: KING OF KINGS AND LORD OF LORDS.
>
> Revelation 19:11–16

This is the God we serve, he with the strong right arm. And this is where we are headed, toward that great day when all will recognize his sovereign authority, power, and majesty.

And this is the promise which is yet being fulfilled: "The LORD said to my Lord, 'Sit at My right hand till I make Your enemies Your footstool'" (Ps. 110:1). The drama comes to its climax not at the incarnation, not at the crucifixion, not even at the resurrection. Rather the crescendo is reached here, when all his enemies are a footstool to him. It is at this time that "every knee [shall] bow, of those in heaven, and of those on earth, and of those under the earth, and that every tongue [shall] confess that Jesus Christ is Lord, to the glory of God the Father" (Phil. 2:10–11).

God is. He is the great "I am." He has been almighty from the beginning. All power stems from him. None have power without his first giving it to them. And he has chosen to exercise that power in the great display of history. We are indeed players upon his stage. But he is no idiot who tells this story. And while he is full of sound and fury, his story signifies not nothing, but he who is everything. We ought to remember that we are here for him, and not he for us. And we ought to be practicing for eternity.

As we look about his world and see the play not yet through, we must focus on the ending. Paul tells us we are even now seated in the heavenlies with Christ Jesus (Eph. 2:6) and our citizenship is in heaven (Phil. 3:20). We should, then, even here, sing with choirs of angels, "Holy, holy, holy, Lord God Almighty, who was and is and is to come!" (Rev. 4:8).

How strong is he? Stronger than all we could ever imagine. How strong was he? Stronger than all that ever was. How strong will he be? Strong enough to bring all things to pass, to conquer every enemy, and to stoop to us who are his children and wipe away every tear.

He is coming. And he will come in all his strength and in all his glory. Even so, come Lord Jesus.

R. C. Sproul Jr. is a pastor of an Associate Reformed Presbyterian church, editor-in-chief of and contributor to *Tabletalk* magazine, and director of the Highlands Study Center in Meadowview, Virginia. He has authored or edited four books, including *Dollar Signs of the Times.*